DRONE
PROFESSIONAL 2

21 professional drone experts
give you their current best thinking
on drone technology, best practice
and business success

*To my great friend Florence Irwin
(Flo) Thanks for All your support
I hope you enjoy the read*

WM

Drone Professional 2

Copyright 2021 W&M Publishing

First published in January 2021

ISBN 978-1-912774-78-4 ebk
ISBN 978-1-912774-79-1 pbk

Editor: Louise Jupp & Andrew Priestley

The rights of Dave Scott, Andre Meredith, Daniel Blomerus, Maayke Leenstra, Kim James, Ian Kiely, Itumeleng Mokoena, Filippo Tomasello, Gift Kgadima, Queen Ndlovu, Dean Polley, Godfrey Nolan, Justin Melman, Debbie Jewitt PhD, Jamie Allan, Clive Mathe, Sonet Kock, Tawanda Chihambakwe, Timothy Wise, Andrew Priestley and Louise Jupp to be identified as contributing authors of this work have been asserted in accordance with Sections 77 and 78 of the Copyright Designs and Patents Act, 1988.

A CIP catalogue record for this book is available from the British Library.

Disclaimer: *Drone Professional 2* is intended for information and education purposes only. This book does not constitute specific legal, financial, health, clinical, commercial or industry advice unique to your situation.

The views and opinions expressed in this book are those of the authors and do not reflect those of the Publisher and Resellers, who accept no responsibility for loss, damage or injury to persons or their belongings as a direct or indirect result of reading this book.

All people mentioned in case studies have been used with permission, and/or have had names, genders, industries and personal details altered to protect client confidentiality.

Every attempt has been made to ensure citations and Copyright usage is accurate and with permission. Please notify us with any errors or omissions and we will rectify in subsequent reprints.

Cover image courtesy of Wingtra.

Contents

5 **Welcome**

9 **Dave Scott**
Evolution and Application:
A Personal Perspective

17 **Andre P Meredith**
Commercial Drone Operations:
Risk Assessment Simplified

29 **Daniel Blomerus**
Drone Insurance 101

37 **Maayke Leenstra**
The Use Of Drones In Shaping A Vital Living
Environment: A Helicopter View

47 **Kim James**
Managing General Insurance Risk From Above

57 **Ian Kiely**
The Accidental Geek – Importance Of Satellites

65 **Itumeleng Mokoena**
The Use of Drone Technology
For Informal Settlement Upgrading

73 **Filippo Tomasello**
UAS Traffic Management (UTM):
What Perspectives For The Future?

85 **Gift Kgadima**
It Takes A Team To Get Airborne

95 **Queen Ndlovu**
Drone Manufacturing Journey –
You Dream It, We Build It!

103 **Dean Polley**
UTM: A Modern Day Wright Brothers Moment

113 **Godfrey Nolan**
What Can AI And Drones Do?

121 **Justin Melman**
Red Lorry, Yellow Lorry And Submarines
In The Sky

133 **Debbie Jewitt PhD**
Best Practice Guidelines For Minimising
Wildlife Disturbance By Drones

141 **Jamie Allan**
UAV Technology Overview
In The Global Energy Industries

153 **Clive Mathe**
Kurai

161 **Sonet Kock**
UAS Categorisation Model Adoption -
A South African Perspective

175 **Tawanda Chihambakwe**
The Power Of Local - How A Global Movement
For Good Is Changing The Drone Industry

185 **Timothy Wise**
Drone Crop Spraying In South Africa

191 **Andrew Priestley**
Marketing Your Commercial Drone Capability

199 **Louise Jupp**
Mind The Gap – The Opportunities The Drone
Industry Offers As A Driver For Closing
The Gender Gap In Aviation

209 **Contribute To Future Editions
Of Drone Professional**

Welcome to Drone Professional 2

This is the second edition in a series of books designed to showcase the value of the wide-ranging applications of drone technology in the hands of the professionals, as presented by the professionals themselves. It follows on the heels of the best-selling *Drone Professional 1*.

Drone Professional 1 has inspired readers to investigate the potential of the drone industry for their own specific professions or requirements. It has provided a practical reference guide on the reality of applying drone technology in a variety of ways. The book has also been instrumental in educating readers on the extensive range of applications, multi-disciplinary collaborations and benefits of drone technology. More importantly, it has created a greater appreciation of the legal and operational standards within which professionals operate and the high standards professionals set for themselves.

As I reflect on the year since *Drone Professional 1* was published, there have been significant developments in unmanned aviation, many of which exemplify the very best benefits drone technology offers to society. Some will also help foster a greater trust in the safe and accountable integration and management of drones in our airspace.

Most notably, the global pandemic has accelerated the development and implementation of drone delivery programmes for essential public service applications.

Some of these programmes are delivering PPE and test kits as well as food parcels for isolated communities or high-risk residents. Other delivery programmes are for more routine services such as medical supply or postal delivery.

Another key development has been the wider adoption of drone technology by first responders for a range of public safety applications, such as for the wildfires in the USA. Their use has provided both expected and unexpected benefits on account of the quantity and quality of mapping data collected before, during and after a wildfire has occurred. The real-time data and processed information has helped to map the path of the fires; identify the 'hotspots' to be targeted by first responders; assess the fire damage caused; and provide information for the future restoration and rebuilding. Significantly, the use of drone technology in these situations has benefitted multiple parties besides the first responders. These include the property owners, town planners and insurance assessors. In Australia, the combination of drone technology, including artificial intelligence, is helping conservationists and wildlife managers assess habitat damage; execute more effective animal rescue programmes; and accelerate forest rehabilitation programmes with seed-planting drone systems after wildfires.

From a more operational perspective, there have been significant developments in unmanned traffic management systems and the adoption of remote IDs for drones. There is progress with harmonising drone regulations across regions as well as more proactive reviews of drone regulations – subjects covered in this edition. All of these operational developments are essential to facilitating the growth of the professional drone industry, but without compromising safety.

I am again delighted to bring together 21 drone industry professionals from around the world for *Drone Professional 2*. They are all specialists in their chosen fields and consummate professionals in the drone community. Collectively they share their experience, insights, best practice guidance and current best thinking on a broad range of subjects in unmanned aviation. *Drone Professional 2* is a global production. The authors hail from around the world including, South Africa, the Netherlands, Ireland, Italy, USA, UK, Zimbabwe and Australia. Their professional experience, best thinking and advice has relevance and value in any geographical location, as does their vision for the drone industry.

I hope you gain new insights on the value of the professional drone industry to society and the range of technologies and innovations that contribute to the industry. I also hope you will appreciate the frameworks and standards within which professionals ply their trade with typical single-minded dedication and vision. Finally, I hope you glimpse the considerable potential the professional drone industry has still to offer in the hands of the professionals.

Enjoy.

Louise Jupp (Editor)

Evolution and Application: A Personal Perspective

Dave Scott

The use of Unmanned Aerial Vehicles (UAVs) is vast and the rate of development is huge. Almost daily there is news of a new company, a model upgrade, or some small or large breakthrough in flight time or payload capacity. It is an exciting time to be involved in such a rapidly growing industry and one which yields fascination to both hobbyists and professionals.

Although born from military purposes, UAV technology has been adopted across the globe for many worthy uses such as firefighting, sea rescue, shark observations, search and rescue, mapping for sustainability, mapping and preserving archaeological sites, assisting to apprehend poachers on land and sea, reforestation efforts, supporting law enforcement, delivering blood and medical supplies to remote areas, reducing the risk of inspections on human lives, and many more.

Applying The Technology

My background into the use of UAVs and associated technology began with a multitude of childhood aviation-related toys and grew into MSc research in Antarctica in the field of geomorphology. Geomorphology is the study of landforms, their processes, form and sediments at the surface of the Earth. Prior to the use of UAV technology researchers used to have to manually measure every aspect of the landscape features, such as diameter, shape, size, slope, aspect, visual notes. Working in an environment such as Antarctica is often a challenge due to the limitations of cold weather clothing coupled with the rapid changing weather conditions. There are often only a couple of hours to collect all of the samples and data before a blizzard moves in. This tends to rush the data collection process and researchers are often forced to leave a study area without obtaining a sufficient data count. This was a challenge personally experienced in the first of my research trips to Antarctica.

On the subsequent voyage, however, we decided to look into using some new UAV technology as part of the project. Two obstacles to be navigated were the fact that no one involved completely understood the UAV technology, and the use of this technology was not part of the initial project funding. Our first UAV *Liewe Heksie* was created on a very tight budget with the express purpose to assist the research project[1]. She was a combination of wood, aluminum, Tupperware and foam, glue, duct tape, elastic bands, cable ties and a bunch of other bits and pieces which joined the show every time a repair was needed.

Initially one challenge was to get the craft to fly well, especially down at those extreme latitudes where satellite connection was intermittent. The craft would often fly off on its own - hence the name *Liewe Heksie*. It soon became apparent that there was an issue with the GPS. After disabling the GPS, all the sampling had to be done in manual flight mode which became a nerve-racking experience. The areas of Antarctica where I was operating were sheer rock and ice and the glare was vicious; keeping visual focus on the UAV flying into the sun was near-blinding. It was a tense flight operation sending the craft over the huge mountain valleys, with me squinting into the distance, mostly flying based on the trust that she was facing the right direction and trying to use sound to figure out whether she was coming closer or not, and sprinting around using the faint squeal of the motors to determine which direction to turn in order to bring the craft back safely. This was indeed an experience and it is not often that one sweats in Antarctica.

Despite the enormous operational challenges of this primitive "UAV", aerial data was collected and significantly boosted the quality of the research project. Within thirty minutes, the entire mountain slope had been mapped and after linking this aerial data with precision GPS marked Ground Control Points (GCPs), I was able to generate an accurate 3-dimensional model of all the landscape features and analyse the full details from the laptop in the comfort of my office. My average samples for statistical analysis went from 10-20 up to well over 100 per site and we now have a digital record for future studies and analytics.

I have since set up a business in the UAV industry, and for many years Caelum Technologies has been developing skills and services for multiple industries. This has resulted in involvement in a number of fascinating projects, some of which have required modelling in five-millimetre-per-pixel resolutions.

The use of UAV technology has revolutionised countless industries and has enabled things that were previously considered impossible.

UAVs And The Future

Although there is amazing technology available already, professionals in the UAV industry are waiting eagerly for that explosive moment when battery technology flips. There is a huge developmental push worldwide to improve the lifespan, capacity and power provided by batteries. This will assist industries across the globe and impact almost everyone in some or other way. Picture this: a battery which weighs only a few kilograms powering a household on a remote island for over a month on a single charge, and paralleled by a small solar panel to keep the battery topped up even in areas where direct sunlight is minimal. Let us allow our imaginations to run wild with the possibilities; smartphones and laptops which last weeks on a single charge, transportation transforming into electric power and becoming affordable for us all, cable-less appliances, and the list goes on. Wouldn't it be amazing to live in a city where the noise and pollution generated from a highway is dramatically reduced?

Once the development in battery power reaches a changing point, the UAV industry will accept the extra flight time with open arms. Flight time on the standard off-the-shelf UAVs is a huge limiting factor and UAV professionals all want more and more flight time. For the last few years it seems that only a few minutes of flight time is added to the craft as the next model comes out. Until the revolution on battery power technology comes along, manufacturers have to be innovative in order to produce UAVs with longer flight times.

The following methods have been used to achieve longer flight times and for a logical system;

- Large crafts have highly efficient motor and propeller set-ups to accommodate the extra battery weight.

- Hybrid multirotors carry a gas-powered generator on board which powers the motors for flight. A battery is on board only in the case of a failure in generator, to bring the craft safely to landing.

- Hydrogen fuel cell powered crafts. These cells usually provide up to three times the flight endurance.

- In hybrid Vertical Take-off and Landing fixed wing UAVs, taking off and landing is done using battery power and then transitioning into forward flight powered by gasoline engines.

Although incredibly innovative technology exists in the UAV industry, the problem remains that these all usually come with a large price tag, increased maintenance complexity and availability, and therefore are limiting to the consumer UAV market.

Working In This Industry

Working in the UAV industry is often understood as flying UAVs all day. This is rarely the case. Job dependent, of course, there is much more that is required. To use Caelum Technologies as an example, the workforce collectively needs to have knowledge and skills in GIS, surveying, mapping, photography, videography, science, R&D, construction of UAVs, as well as the operation of UAVs.

UAVs and their applications are becoming more and more autonomous as this generally yields a better result for data collection than in manual flight. As an example, a project to collect overlapping images of a tower based on an autonomous helical flight mission is likely to collect the correct quality and quantity of imagery in comparison to a manual flight mission. In fact, in manual flight it is likely that too many images are collected and this in turn may impact the productivity of the entire work flow.

The implications of this for an aspiring UAV pilot are that his/her job becomes more of a monitoring process than a hands-on skilled UAV pilot. But then again, if in the event of a GPS glitch or some or other failure, the pilot should be more than capable of applying their skills to bring the craft safely back down to ground.

Not to be ignored is the legal framework for UAV operations stipulated by your country. Although they may be frustrating, they have been put in place for good reasons. Becoming a professional involves all aspects of this technology and the legal operations are a key component of this, as ultimately this will earn the respect of your clients and be the catalyst for the formation of long term business relationships.

UAVs and associated technology has been booming over the years and is still in its infancy stage. It is a fascinating and exciting area to be involved in and is rapidly expanding and constantly opening new opportunities for researchers and business.

Reference

1. *Liewe Heksie* (Little Witch) is a South African TV series I used to watch as a child and centred around a witch who used to fly off on her broomstick. So when the UAV used to be out of control and doing its own thing, it reminded me of this series and one of my childhood memories.

About Dave Scott

Dave Scott (BSc, BSc H, MSc) first became involved with unmanned aerial systems during his MSc research in the field of geomorphology. The topic of his research based dissertation is *On active layer processes and landforms in Western Dronning Maud Land, Antarctica*. Due to the remoteness of Antarctica it became obvious that a special system was needed to collect valuable aerial data.

He designed and built an autonomous multirotor which could withstand the harsh Antarctica temperatures and conditions. The system was able to collect high quality 2-dimensional and 3-dimensional photograghs, indisputably a beneficial tool in the aid of this scientific research.

Since completing his Masters dissertation, Dave Scott has dedicated his time to designing, building and utilizing UAVs to capture aerial images and create accurate 3-dimensional models. Dave is the CEO and Co-Founder of Caelum Technologies (Pty) Ltd, a Remote Sensing company offering services across South Africa and Africa as a whole.

Contacts

www.caelumtech.co.za

https://www.linkedin.com/in/dave-scott-514b5a127

https://www.facebook.com/caelumtechnologies

dave.scott@caelumtech.co.za

Commercial Drone Operations: Risk Assessment Simplified

Andre P. Meredith

Ever since the DJI Phantom I was launched in January 2013, drones have proliferated to the point where they have almost become household appliances. This observation applies predominantly to the recreational sphere, but the commercial drone environment has also grown in leaps and bounds, and new uses – including equally novel designs – are emerging almost on a weekly basis. The potential for unmanned aircraft seems almost limitless.

Of course, along with this explosive growth comes the potential for increased operation in controlled airspace and over built up areas, including densely populated towns and cities. The proliferation of drones, along with improvements in technology, is paving the way for longer flight times, increasing exposure to hazards and an increased time-at-risk, which is especially dangerous if the risk level is high.

Most drone professionals understand the need to assess operational risk prior to any form of flight (including ground runs and launching / recovery phases). The challenge remains: how to assess risk in a way that is systematic and thorough, yet simplified to the point where regular operators can perform it consistently and reliably.

This write-up proposes an approach to address risk assessments in a manner that can be applied to regular, steady-state commercial drone operations, as well as to flight involving experimental (in-development) drones. With minor tailoring to the use-case, the approach can be applied to virtually any drone operation.

The 5M Risk Assessment Model

Originally developed for the manned commercial aviation industry[1, 2], the 5M Model can be applied to the commercial drone industry with equal aplomb, albeit with some tweaking to cater for increased attention to protection of third parties. The 5M Risk Assessment Model essentially requires that hazards be identified, and their effects be considered, within the five primary building blocks of any drone operation:

- M1: The Mission. The type of work (job, mission or task) the drone will be doing.

- M2: The Medium. The physical, electromagnetic and climatic environment within which the drone will be operating.

- M3: Management. The support functions, documentation, processes and procedures having a bearing on the drone operation.

- M4: The Man. The operating and technical support organisation, including key people having major impact on safety of flight.

- M5: The Machine. The actual drone and critical ground support systems (command, control and telemetry/status, radio links, launch and recovery, storage, etc).

It is to be expected that there will be some overlap between some of these building blocks. For example, it may be difficult to split the Mission and the Medium, and certain managerial and organisational aspects may also be tough to categorise, creating some grey area between Management and Man. The important factor to keep in mind is that exact categorisation is not critical; as long as the hazard has been identified for assessment.

Risk Assessment Process

Aviation risk needs to be determined, quantified and mitigated if deemed unacceptable. This is the cornerstone of proactive aviation safety. There are many standards [3, 4, 5, 6], that can be consulted to shed light on the aforementioned, but this article aims to present a model that should be fairly easy for most commercial drone operators to apply. The Risk Assessment process contains seven key steps. The first step in this process is the identification of hazards. It then follows a fairly logical process where causes are identified, probabilities and severities are attributed, end effects are derived, risks levels are calculated and mitigations are developed (if required). The diagram below provides a visual depiction of this process:

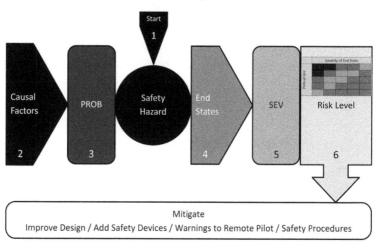

Figure 1: 7-Step Risk Assessment Process

The process above is based on the simplified Bow-Tie assessment model, requiring identification of hazards, then identification of threats or causal factors that could energise the hazard, identification of consequences or end states once energised, and then finding solutions to prevent this from occurring. The starting point is in the middle of the bow-tie:

Figure 2: Simplified Bow-Tie Assessment Model

Further details concerning the process are as follows:

Step 1: Identify Safety Hazards

Note that hazards are not accidents in and of themselves. Accidents are caused by hazards. In turn, hazards are created by failures, omissions, faults (contributing factors) called Causal Factors (CF).

Step 2: Determine Causal Factors

These are any factors potentially leading to the creation of the Hazard.

Step 3: Attribute Probabilities Of Occurrence

Allocate a Probability of Occurrence to each CF. The following probability levels may be used to classify the likelihood that a hazard will materialise:

5	Certain		So likely it can be assumed it *will happen* during the mission or flight. It is also likely to occur more than once or regularly. It is known to have occurred before, and quite frequently or regularly.
4	High		There is a *strong* chance that it might happen during the mission or flight. It is likely to occur at times. It has occurred before, but infrequently.
3	Occasional		There is a *reasonable* chance that it might happen during the mission or flight. Unlikely, but could possibly occur. It has occurred on rare occasions.
2	Low		There is a *very slim* chance that it might happen during the mission or flight. It is not known to have occurred before.
1	Unlikely		So unlikely that it can be considered it *will never* happen during the mission or flight. Almost inconceivable that it will occur.

Figure 3: Probabilities of Occurrence

The most conservative level should always be selected if there is any uncertainty (as an example, if there is uncertainty if a probability of occurrence would be Low or Occasional, then Occasional should be selected).

Step 4: Determine End State

Determine the worst-case End State (end result) should the Hazard materialise.

Step 5: Attribute Severities

Allocate a Severity Level to the End State, per CF. The following severity levels may be used to classify the severity of the outcome (End State), once the Hazard has materialised.

5	Catastrophic		An Outcome that can result in: • Death to people • Total destruction of private property • Total destruction of the aircraft • Irrecoverable damage to the environment
4	Hazardous		An Outcome that can result in: • Severe injury to people (permanent loss of function) • Severe damage to private property (requiring major reconstruction) • Severe damage to the aircraft (requiring major investment to repair) • Severe damage to the environment (recoverable over a long period) This condition is usually accompanied by severely increased workload, to the extent that the individuals carrying out the work (e.g. the remote pilot) cannot be relied upon to safety continue carrying out tasks.
3	Major		An Outcome that can result in: • Injury to people (requiring some form of medical attention) • Damage to private property (requiring repairs) • Damage to the aircraft (requiring some investment to repair) • Damage to the environment (recoverable over a moderate period) This condition is usually accompanied by increased workload, to the extent that the individuals carrying out the work (e.g. the remote pilot) have difficulty to cope with the new conditions.
2	Minor		An Outcome that can result in: • Minor injury to people (slight lacerations) • Minor damage to private property (superficial only) • Minor damage to the aircraft (requiring minimal investment to repair) • Minor damage to the environment (recoverable over a short period) This condition is usually accompanied by slightly increased workload (e.g. for the remote pilot) due to some form of operational or procedural deviation.
1	No Effect		An Outcome that can result in: • No injury to people • No damage to private property • No damage to the aircraft • No damage to the environment An operational nuisance only.

Figure 4: Severity of End State

The most conservative level should always be selected if there is any uncertainly (as an example, if there is uncertainty if an End State severity should be considered as Minor or Major, then Major should be selected).

The potential workload increase may be used as an additional measure to help determine the applicable severity level.

Step 6: Calculate Risk Levels

Risk is the combination of the Probability of Occurrence of

Risk Matrix						
		Severity				
		Catastrophic (5)	Hazardous (4)	Major (3)	Minor (2)	No Effect (1)
Probability	Certain (5)	25	20	15	10	5
	High (4)	20	16	12	8	4
	Occasional (3)	15	12	9	6	3
	Low (2)	10	8	6	4	2
	Unlikely (1)	5	4	3	2	1

Figure 5: Risk Matrix

The Risk Matrix above may be tailored as required.

The Risk Level is determined by mapping the estimated Probability of Occurrence with the perceived end state Severity. The Risk Level is determined by considering the risk score, as follows:

Risk Score	Risk Level	Mitigation Level of Effort
1 to 6	Low Risk	Acceptable risk, no additional mitigation required.
7 to 12	Medium Risk	Must be controlled through internal training, heightened crew awareness and minor adjustments to company operating procedures, as required.
13 to 18	High Risk	Must be fully mitigated either by design, safety devices, warning devices, operational limitations/restrictions, or by additional organisational procedures. Mitigation must be tested before being accepted into Company Procedures. Mitigation must be approved by either Responsible Person Flight Operations or Responsible Person Technical, depending on area affected.
19 to 25	Extreme Risk	Must be fully mitigated either by design, safety devices, warning devices, operational limitations/restrictions, or by additional organisational procedures. Mitigation must be tested before being accepted into Company Procedures. Mitigation must be approved by the CEO/Accountable Manager.

Figure 6: Risk Levels

This an important step; after all, it would be a waste of time to go through the entire assessment without rectifying unacceptable risks. The Level of Effort required for mitigation of the various risks identified will be commensurate with that specified in the table above. Mitigations developed by steady-state operators (commercial operators) will most likely be procedural adaptations, additional training, specific competence, organisational or managerial changes, and the like. Drone system developers have the additional advantage in that they can make design changes or add warnings (in software) to remote pilots.

The Risk Assessment process should be applied within each of the five building blocks (M1 to M5). To put it simply, consider which hazards would be found within the ambit of the Mission. Then consider any hazards associated with the Medium within which the operation will take place. Thereafter consider any Managerial-centric hazards, as well as hazards associated with the people, especially the Remote Pilot. Finally, consider any hazards attributable to the drone system itself (largely technical).

An important factor to keep in mind while performing the Risk Assessment and determining severity of the End State is to always be mindful of the operating environment. As an example: a drone experiencing a failure whilst being operated at low altitude over farmland, far from third parties and within relatively sterile airspace, will exhibit a much lower Severity of End State than the same drone experiencing the same failure whilst being operated over built-up areas or in controlled airspace. The former will lead to a lower risk level, and may require no mitigation, whilst the latter will exhibit much higher risk levels, requiring robust mitigation.

It should be noted that if this process is applied within a test / experimental / drone development scenario, much of the risk is automatically reduced (auto-mitigated) if the test flights are constrained to a test area with a predefined Safety Footprint. The Safety Footprint is, of course, three-dimensional, and includes not only a sterile terrestrial area, but also sterile airspace. It goes without saying that systems or process need to be in place to ensure that the drone will stay within the defined Safety Footprint in this case.

The entire Risk Assessment process can be streamlined through the use of templates. Having a known format will make it easier for both drone operators performing the assessment and regulators evaluating the results. This would also be beneficial for non-aviators entering the drone operations environment, having no background in aviation risk assessments.

Conclusion

It is common knowledge that aviation is risky by its very nature. Drones are aircraft in their own right (albeit devoid of onboard pilots) operating in airspace shared with other manned aircraft. The removal of the pilot from the cockpit is but one of many unique attributes, making drone-related flight operations theoretically riskier than manned aviation. This necessitates a structured operational risk assessment for drone operations to ensure that drone flight remains hazard-controlled.

To put it simply: if you fail to plan, then you plan to fail. If hazards are known they can be managed. A structured risk assessment program is the key.

Drones have been categorised as *disruptive technology*, with significant attention being given to the novelty of solutions and system adaptability. The world is becoming ever more automated, and fully-autonomous drone operations are probably not far off. Autonomous Air Taxi development is also speeding ahead. A structured risk assessment program will be a critical factor to enable and guarantee safe commercial drone flight operations into the future.

References

1. K., Cusick, Stephen; T., Wells, Alexander (2012). Commercial aviation safety. McGraw-Hill Professional.

2. Stolzer, A.J.; Goglia, J.J. Safety management systems in aviation.

3. ARP 4761, Guidelines and Methods for Conducting the Safety Assessment Process on Civil Airborne Systems and Equipment.

4. Federal Aviation Regulation Part 23 paragraph 1309, Equipment, Systems and Installations.

5. European Aviation Safety Agency Certification Standard 23 paragraph 1309, Equipment, Systems and Installations.

6. British Standard European Norm (BS EN) 61508 Part 5 Annex B, Functional safety of electrical/electronic/programmable electronic safety related systems.

About Andre P. Meredith

Andre Meredith completed his Bachelor of Mechanical Engineering degree at the University of Stellenbosch in 1994 and obtained a Master of Science in Engineering degree at the University of Stellenbosch in 2011, having performed research into the feasibility of utilising large drones for long range maritime search and rescue. He has been employed in the South African Air  Force since 1990 and has served in various positions, including design engineering, engineering management, project engineering, system engineering and finally certification of military air systems.

He is currently Acting Director System Integrity, where he has been serving since 2008. Responsibilities include technical airworthiness oversight and type certification of military air systems, including military drones (twelve types to date, including Type Certification of a 650kg MALE drone).

In addition to his military duties he is performing part-time safety consultation to operators of commercial drones, enabling them to apply for flight clearance certificates. He soon identified the need for structured safety guidance to commercial and recreational drone operators, leading to the development and publication of his first book entitled *The Drone Safety Handbook*.

He is currently an Associate at Avior Labs (Pty) Ltd.

Contacts

https://www.mysafedrone.co.za

https://aviorlabs.com

https://www.linkedin.com/in/andre-meredith-13b63a26

andrepm32@gmail.com

Drone Insurance 101

Daniel Blomerus

Note: The intent of this article is for the licensed commercial Drone operator and not that of a recreational or hobby operator.

Insurance; never the most popular of topics. However, by way of example I want to explain drone insurance and how, as a drone professional, you are at risk if this is not a priority on your safety checklist.

Imagine this scenario, you have been asked to survey agricultural farmland used for growing sugarcane before the crop sprayers are initiated to spray pesticide. You start by unpacking your DJI Matrice 210 with a Zenmuse X7, a drone very well designed to do a quick survey of the area and process the data in a fast and cost-effective way. The landowner gives you permission, and the Local Aviation Authority grants your approvals. You have completed your Remote Pilots Licence (RPL) and made sure all your safety checks are completed. You initiate 'start' and the drone continues the pre-set flight path you have selected.

All is well in the day of the Professional drone pilot; but what if the day deviates for the worse and there is an accident?

As unreal as it might sound the fact of the matter is cyber-crime is on the rise and you, as the drone operator, could be in danger of interceptors and hackers trying to manipulate your drone.

Imagine: The drone collides with the powerline transformer and causes an explosion. Your drone is wrecked and all the data you collected is destroyed. You took out drone insurance and luckily you are covered for accidental damage to your drone.

The Reason For Drone Hull And Payload Insurance

Most aviation insurers offer a complete solution for professional drone operators and because of the high costs of the specialized equipment, you need to make sure that your asset(s) are correctly insured.

The industry is evolving quickly and for some operators it is difficult to keep up. Most of the larger drone manufacturers are giving the operators the ability to interchange different payloads, such as the LiDAR sensors, multi spectral and photogrammetry cameras. The fact is the equipment does not form part of your drone's hull but is rather seen as part of the payload. The definition of hull coverage in insurance terms has been taken from manned aircraft as a common type of insurance that covers the owners of aircraft against loss resulting from damage to their craft. This has been implemented in the drone underwriting wordings.

The insurers take this information into account when rating the risk on your operation. We see a lot of clients in the Industry operate with one drone but have three or four different payloads. It is important to ask your Insurer about this and how they will calculate your premiums.

With the DJI Matrice 210 you could only attach two cameras at a time, meaning all your equipment will not be at risk of flying all the time. The premium should be rated accordingly and not all as one total accumulated risk. This is an industry conundrum as most insurers do not see these as items or equipment, but as a single unit, which means that you (as the insured) will be paying more on your own insurance.

Imagine: As the drone collides with the transformer it cuts the power line and sends the drone crashing to the ground. Your drone becomes an unstoppable fire ball because of the highly flammable lithium batteries. The now uncontrollable firenado of a drone falls into the mostly dry sugar cane plantation and starts an overpowering inferno. The landowner rushes to the field and deploys his fire rescue team to assist in stopping the fire. As the fire gets under control the estimated yield lost is around 4 hectares (9.8 acres). The landowner holds you, the drone professional, liable for the damage and loss of crop caused by the fire.

General Liability and Aviation Third Party Insurance - What is the Difference?

Aviation Third Party Liability Insurance is a specialized offering and not one that all insurers want to offer. The reason being that the exposure is far greater than your Standard General Liability Insurance. The major difference between third party drone insurance and general liability is that the drone third party wording is specifically worded to provide cover for the drone industry and its applicable regulations. However, the general liability wording has specific exclusions concerning any business activities where drones are associated with or conducted on.

The case maybe fought that your drone was hacked and that caused the drone to collide with the powerline. However, the ruling may be turned around that you were the pilot in control and that your drone caused the accident. The consequential damages are those of the sugar cane field that are now destroyed. Sufficient liability limits need to be looked at when conducting any drone operations. The pilot flying over open land has a far lesser risk than that of a videographer filming the new Bond film. We, as insurers, look at the specific type of risk involved and try and assist client(s) in selecting the sufficient liability limits.

Imagine: You register your claim with your insurer and because you had the correct paperwork in place, and were in complete control of the drone before the hack occurred, your claim is processed under the Hull & Payload Insurance. You had also selected a higher than the standard Liability Limit and you have Cyber Liability selected as additional cover which means you are covered for the possible hack. You, as the professional drone pilot, are covered under your insurance and could replace your equipment and pay the damages towards the farmer.

Remember that safety comes first when operating your drone. No matter where you are in the world you must consider the airspace you are flying in and the regulations you must adhere to. When selecting the insurer, always ask these questions and use this case study as an example of a claim, no matter how realistic you might find it, to choose the correct insurance that suits you.

References

1. The Civil Aviation Authority of Botswana (2016) Operation of Remotely Piloted Aircraft, Bye-Law 07 of 2016, [online], available: https://www.caab.co.bw/wp-content/uploads/Bye-Law-07-of-2016-Operation-of-Remotely-Piloted-Aircraft (if this site does not work try: https://www.droneregulations.info/Botswana/BW.html)

2. Morgan, S. (2020) Special Report: Cyberwarfare In The C-Suite. Cybercrime To Cost The World $10.5 Trillion Annually By 2025, Cybercrime Magazine, [online], available: https://cybersecurityventures.com/cybercrime-damages-6-trillion-by-2021

3. Kamkar, S. (2013) Skyjack , [online], available: http://samy.pl/skyjack

About Daniel Blomerus

Daniel is a Drone Insurance specialist and a forerunner of drone insurance in South Africa. He has been in the insurance industry for 14 years and started looking at drones and the insurance thereof in 2015. A good friend introduced him to an Industry that from that day changed his life. Today he is a leading broker for drone insurance in South Africa and has made it his mission to understand the South African Civil Aviation Authority Rules and Regulations set out for drone operators. He partnered with an insurer in writing a comprehensive drone insurance product to assist the commercial drone operator specifically with a holistic approach on their insurance needs. Daniel assists by identifying trends and compiling data to assess claims by ways of flight logs and data collected from the drone. By processing the data received from the drone he can explain the cause of accident and protect the pilot in control as well as the insurer against fraudulent claims. Daniel has a passion for the Industry and what drones can do to protect and save lives.

Contacts

https://www.linkedin.com/in/daniel-j-blomerus-273670189/

Daniel@unicorninsurance.co.za

The Use Of Drones In Shaping A Vital Living Environment: A Helicopter View

Maayke Leenstra

As a Geospatial Data consultant working for an environmental consultancy firm, I spend my days working in ecology, soil and groundwater research, noise studies, site development, construction and hydrological studies. As such, I have the privilege to work with all kinds of geospatial data, within a variety of different fields, generated by a variety of different sources. I tend to look at drones from a (geospatial) data perspective. Simply put, I would not introduce myself so much as a drone professional, but rather as a Geospatial Data professional who has worked with a variety of drone data.

A Digital Front Runner

So, as an environmental consultancy firm, where do we fit in? What is our role and incentive in drones? Before diving into this, it is useful to grasp what our business entails. It boils down to this: we help our clients in shaping a vital living environment by providing impactful solutions within a variety of themes - think sustainability, water, infrastructure and soil and groundwater.

In order to do so, a large part of our business is dedicated to collecting data and consulting based upon it. Having been like this for over half a century, one could argue that data collection, data analysis and data consultancy runs through our veins. Yet, with the rise of new digital tools and technologies, the circumstances under which we collect data and consult are changing. We believe that a strong link exists between digitalisation and sustainability. As such, in order to shape a vital living environment, we need to be a digital front runner in the use and application of data-based technologies.

So, one can probably imagine that devices that allow our sensors to go air bound, naturally open up a lot of interesting opportunities!

Equipping drones with a variety of sensors opens the way for all kinds of applications, ranging from ecological inspections to air quality (chimney) measurements. What do these different applications have in common? The use of drones can lead to improved safety, increased efficiency and an increase in the amount of data that is being captured.

Since our objective is to get the most out of the collected data, we need to know which remote sensing technique works best for the project at hand. But our job certainly does not stop at knowing how to best collect the data: transforming it into information and consecutively translating it into knowledge and advice is what it's all about! On top of that, we need to be able to consult our clients about the additional opportunities that arise from the collected data.

Flying Cameras

Drones are popularly seen as 'just' flying cameras. Personally, I would rather have them be seen as flying sensors. All these different sensors can generate a whole lot of meaningful data. Yet even the opportunities that a drone generates by being 'just' a flying camera, are already quite astonishing.

'Just' the RGB sensor (i.e. the camera) can create tons of

information that is of great value within our daily work! Since the RGB sensor is capable of quickly mapping large areas (more and more accurately) in 3D by generating point clouds, it opens up a wide range of options, now and in the future.

Though there are a few devices that are capable of creating point clouds, drones are currently often favored over other techniques because of their efficiency. Why 'currently', you might ask? Well, that is because there are a few competitors on the horizon for those neat flying cameras! You will read a bit more about the competitors later on in this chapter (see *Hype Or Here To Stay?*).

Now, it would be impossible to list all the opportunities that arise from the use of point clouds within our work. Understanding the general concept of a point cloud is quite essential to the next paragraph.

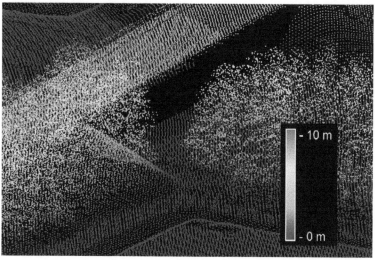

Simply put, a point cloud is a type of data that represents a 3D object through known X, Y and Z coordinates (and its RGB colour value). Point clouds can be generated through a variety of different devices, such as (mobile) laser scanners, LiDAR airplanes, smartphones and drones. For drones, point clouds can either be generated employing the RGB sensor using a methodology called photogrammetry, or by equipping a drone with a LiDAR system.

- **Hydrological Analyses Of Rural, Remote And Urban Areas**
  A point cloud allows us to derive a Digital Terrain Model (DTM).
  DTMs are used to perform hydrological analyses. By determining
  the way water behaves at a project site, these analyses help
  to make project sites more climate proof, quantify the impact
  of new developments on the hydrological cycle and can help
  determine pollutant mobility.
  Note: it depends on the characteristics of the project site (think
  size and vegetation cover) whether using a Real-time Kinematic
  (RTK) drone with an RGB sensor could suffice for this purpose,
  or if using a LiDAR system would be preferable.

- **Digital Sightline And Viewshed Analyses**
  Having a detailed 3D map of a location means we will be able to
  perform a so-called 'sightline' or 'viewshed' analysis. Simply put,
  those analyses enable us to identify what one is able to see,
  from any specific location within that 3D map.
  This valuable information can be used for different purposes,
  such as improving safety (e.g. at traffic interceptions), urban
  design (e.g. fitting in wind turbines) and architecture
  (e.g. determining the best view).

- **Digital Twins**
  In information management, 3D is hot. Specifically, having an up-to-date digital replica of your physical project site, or 'digital twin', is hot. For our industrial clients, safety, health and efficiency are high on the agenda. Having a digital twin for complex sites can improve all of those aspects. The 3D environment can be used for training, sightline analyses and having a real-time helicopter view of the site. Drones are often used to generate the point cloud that is at the base of this helicopter view.

A Technology Constantly Evolving

Now of course, if we would really want to take the opportunities listed above to the next level, the progression does not only depend on the widening of legislation, but also heavily on the advancements in both hard- and software.

In my opinion, the past few years have shown that this is really not something to worry about. Here are two examples that are illustrative of how fast both hard- and software can advance:

- When we first started using drones for 3D mapping, one of the main disadvantages of using a drone was the need for Ground Control Points (GCPs). Needing to be measured physically at (often hard-to-reach) locations, GCPs would really slow down the data collection process.

Fast forward a few years, and the first drones with built-in RTK positioning systems enter the market. The built-in RTK system reduces the need for GCPs to just a handful or even zero GCPs (depending on the application), ultimately making the 3D mapping process more cost-efficient and accurate.

- Back in 2017, it was considered innovative to equip a drone

with an infrared (IR) sensor. To perform comprehensive thermal analysis of a given area with a drone, it required an expensive thermal camera to be (manually) mounted onto a drone.
It also required two drone pilots: one for controlling the drone and its RGB camera, and one for controlling the IR camera, so the data transformation and analyses were challenging.

Fast forward about a year, and the first drones equipped with both RGB and IR sensors (mounted parallelly) enter the market, requiring one pilot and less intensive data transformation techniques. In addition to the upgraded hardware, the software for transforming the collected data also upgraded, making way for automations of processes.

From detecting leakage in pipes to assisting with ecological field research, and from detecting erosion channels below dykes to locating missing persons: it has become clear that built-in IR sensors open the way for a whole new range of applications.

A Cycle Of Enhancement

As Louise Jupp wrote in *Drone Professional 1* (2020), I too believe that drones could significantly change this world, much like aviation did. On a smaller scale, I believe that drones will significantly impact our work as an environmental consultancy. Not only directly, because of the valuable information that can be generated, but also indirectly, by enhancing and complementing other technologies.

Since this is more of a mutually beneficial relationship, I would rather call it a cycle of enhancement.

Some examples include:

• For Virtual Reality (VR), advanced 3D mapping allows for easily creating a 3D replica of any given area. This means that areas do not have to be manually modelled for creating a virtual environment. An accurate depiction of the real-world setting is often crucial to the VR experience, whether it be for safety training for employees at industrial sites, or for experiencing 3D designs with stakeholders.

Conversely, VR goggles for drone pilots can improve the efficiency of visual inspections.

- For spatial Augmented Reality (AR), on the other hand, having an accurate 3D model of the surroundings can take AR experiences to the next level (Mixed Reality (MR)), because it opens the way for occlusion. Occlusion is best explained through the pictures below. Simply put, through the use of an accurate point cloud, the AR device can determine whether a design is in front or behind the physical objects surrounding you. This spatial perception is crucial for using spatial AR in sightline analyses and stakeholder participation.

Conversely, drones benefit from AR and MR through projecting flight lines and other sensors' data over the video image being transmitted from the drone. By being able to see, for example, both video and air quality measurements at the same time while inspecting a chimney, one is able to locate and analyze anomalies more quickly.

Hype Or Here To Stay?

In *Drone Professional 1* (2020), my colleague Jasper Schmeits wrote about the rise of other remote sensing techniques and specifically data collection using satellites. I would not be surprised if - for some of the current drone applications - satellites will be, indeed, the drone's biggest contestants. The rapid hard- and software advancements as described above, are of course also happening on that side of the remote sensing spectrum. As a consequence, the quality, availability and resolution of satellite data is also rising.

For now, drones have the obvious advantage (when flown near the surface) of being able to capture objects 'from below'. They of course also have their resolution in their favor. As such, I would not say that drones and satellites are currently competitive, but rather they are complementary. But with those rapid developments within satellite technology, it might only be a matter of time before satellites can compete with drones in some areas.

This could open up a whole new debate: satellites capturing all kinds of data at a high resolution are arguably safer, but drones (and drone flight paths) are easier to regulate when it comes to privacy.

On the short term, I see commercial airplanes equipped with LiDAR systems as the main competitor for the use of drones in collecting point clouds. Over the past few years, there has been a rise in companies dedicated to LiDAR data collection. They fly airplanes equipped with LiDAR systems regularly over large areas, and make the collected point cloud available in a Data as a Service (DaaS) manner.

So, are drones a hype, or are they here to stay? Although there are some competitors on their horizon, I would definitely not think of drones as a hype. For some applications, I think drones are here to stay. For other applications, they might - in time - be defeated by other remote sensing techniques.

To be frank, for us, this does not really matter: the lessons learned from the use of drones, as well as the advancements it drives in other technologies, are just as valuable as the technique itself!

About Maayke Leenstra

Maayke Leenstra is a Geospatial Data consultant working for the international consultancy and engineering firm TAUW. Her interest for Geographic Information Systems (GIS) and geospatial data was sparked while getting her degree in Earth, Energy and Sustainability. Coming from a multidisciplinary background, she was inspired by the integral and connective value of geospatial data.

In her role as a Geospatial Data consultant at TAUW, she combines her general knowledge of the living environment with her specific knowledge on geospatial data collection, transformation and analysis. In doing so, she aims to solve both environmental and societal challenges by providing data-driven and technology-based solutions. She consults clients on the use of drones, she takes the technical lead in the transformation and analysis of drone data and she is involved with the strategy formation regarding the use of drones within TAUW.

Contacts

Maayke.leenstra@tauw.com

https://www.linkedin.com/in/maayke-leenstra

www.tauw.com

Managing General Insurance Risk From Above

Kim James

There is hardly a forum these days which does not include discussions about drone applications and how these are replacing dull, dirty, and dangerous jobs. At the same time, the drone industry, particularly in the South African context, is figuring out ways to innovate, grow and create new jobs, notwithstanding the perceived ease of accessibility to commercial benefits from this cutting-edge technology. In addition, the effectiveness of drone applications to enhance industry offerings in ways never considered, does not go amiss.

This is where some of the most interesting industry applications come into play. Applications which solve real challenges and extend the impact of digitisation in new and unanticipated ways.

One industry taking advantage of drone technology to enhance its ways of working and improve its own products to benefit the entire value proposition, is General Insurance. The industry is abuzz with how risk managers, insurers and loss adjusters are planning to use, or are already benefitting from Unmanned Aerial Vehicles (UAVs), otherwise known as drones. This is in their quest to enhance risk assessment for underwriting purposes, investigations at claims stage and catastrophe losses, among others.

Assessing The Risk

Traditionally, risk managers used old school methods at the underwriting stage to understand and measure the likelihood and severity of a particular risk occurring. For significantly sized commercial policies for example, this would include reviewing an organisation's safety practices and incident records, insurance claims history, overall health of the business, type of business and the physical state of the plant, equipment and property. This could also include assessing the site's proximity to geographical and neighbouring property risks. Risk managers would review all elements objectively and subjectively given their level of expertise and experience in a particular sector.

This would ordinarily involve physical site inspections, meetings with management, as well as observing parts of the operation on site and taking photographs or video recording for reference. All of this could take days of manual review and capture, not to mention vast distances that often must be covered on foot in the case of a large industrial site. Essentially, the job of the risk manager is to observe and then 'describe' the client site and associated risks in as much detail as possible so as to 'paint' a picture of what is to be insured with its associated risks to the underwriter. The observation part of this exercise of course, has traditionally been done from a human eye-level perspective.

Enter Drones...

Now imagine enhancing those processes with an aerial site model of the premises which captures every viewpoint, feature, and safety hazard through an objective and unbiased lens.

Specific focus can be put on identified parts of a large sophisticated and hazardous plant. Historically these elements would not have been featured in the risk report and perhaps various assumptions would have been made given the physical inaccessibility of things like roof structures, tops of chimneys, flare stacks and furnaces.

The outputs from data obtained using drones to assess commercial or industrial sites, include:

- **Point of interest videos** (using a sophisticated positioning system which puts the drone on an automated flight path around a specific object, while rotating the drone to keep the object centred in the camera frame)

- **3D models** of certain structures (combining multiple overlapping aerial images of the same feature to create digital spatial models)

- **Orthomosaic images** (vertically downward view) of the entire plant, scaled and geographically corrected

- **Thermal images**

- **Close-up videos and images** of specific areas which require closer inspection, using zoom cameras

- **Topographic surveys** to capture detailed site maps, including contours and terrain

This data is obtained through the deployment of a certified and insured drone operator, usually engaged by the risk management organisation conducting the risk assessment of their client's site. However, this is not simply a case of a drone pilot turning up to a site with a drone under his or her arm. There are numerous regulatory, safety, equipment, and process considerations before the first flight can begin.

It goes without saying, the drone operator must be able to obtain all relevant permissions including Flexible Use of Airspace (FUA) permissions in controlled or restricted airspace, as relevant. The pre-site risk assessment will determine any obvious hazards the drone crew will have to take into consideration when planning each of the flights which would then be validated once on site.

Then there is a key requirement to have the right equipment. If the risk manager requires high definition (HD) close-up images, then a high specification zoom camera is required. The requirement might also include thermal data, in which case, depending on what the thermal data is used to assess, a specific type of thermal sensor would be necessary.

Often, large sites mean there are no battery charging facilities, and again, requirements determine the number of flights which may result in many hours of flying. This necessitates the drone crew being prepared with enough charged batteries for the drone/s and all equipment, including controllers.

The risk manager would have already been on their client site for a day or so before the drone crew arrives and in addition to the original brief, might already have determined some risk in an area of the site they would want the drone crew to take a 'closer look at'.

The drone crew generally spends one or two days on site depending on the size and complexity of the task at hand. Complexities include things like a compact site with solid and high metal structures which could make having Radio Line of Site (RLOS) a challenge. In one instance, it necessitated the Pilot in Command (PIC) to climb up a five-story metal staircase to get enough height to obtain RLOS.

Another example was an active flare stack (used for burning off flammable gas) on a large manufacturing plant site, which required careful waypoint flight planning to ensure flight legs not only cleared the height of the 'hazard', but also that the drone did not fly directly over the flare and potentially be incinerated.

Once the flights are complete, specific software is used to translate that data into efficient and easily accessible information, which is usually processed on site and made available to the risk manager immediately. And this is where the insurance industry is benefiting exponentially.

The efficiency and accuracy with which the data is obtained and shared is ground-breaking and depending on the complexity of the client site, this would in most instances save significant person hours and ultimately costs in the first instance.

Data Is King

The real benefit is realised when observations are made once the drone data is reviewed by the risk manager. This is of course in addition to the work already done in the on-site, manual risk assessment process. Understanding potential risks include but are not limited to:

- The state of roof structures including pin-point accuracy of roof and building deterioration, unusual wear and tear, damage caused by windblown debris and organic growth issues

- Security risks given the proximity to nearby neighbourhoods or areas

- Potential on-site hazards

- Slope analysis to determine potential risks in the case of spills or floods

- Risks posed by hazards in neighbouring properties

- Thermal imaging can identify hidden hot spots in pipelines carrying or expelling steam, oil and potential leaks and damp areas

Drone technology supports more accurate actuarial risk assessment and therefore competitive pricing to give customers a better value proposition. By using this real-time drone-collected data, it ultimately drives accurate underwriting and client portfolio management. Most importantly, the client can mitigate any identified risks, the policy adjusted accordingly, and the premium right sized in annual renewal scenarios. For clients who insure large fast-moving inventories or stockpiles, drones are deployed to produce real time volumetric measurements, asset counts and time-spaced comparisons.

Importantly, drone technology used during post loss processes, makes for more accurate loss adjustment, and prevents fraudulent claims. This is to say that in the case of a claim, existing HD geo-tagged images of insured risks can be compared to a post loss drone inspection and only actual new damage or loss compensated for.

Likewise, time-efficiency and accuracy are highlighted again in having a 360-degree birds' eye view of a larger scale claim event or disaster site. Think large scale claim events like floods or industrial site explosions. Drone crews can be deployed at short notice and can assess sites from a physical position of safety, with real time data provided to loss adjusters for claims assessment and proactive client response. When claims can potentially run into hundreds of millions of Rands, it is important to have accurate, independent data.

The volumes of additional data collected through drone imagery is significant. This enriches existing data sets to improve big data analytic capabilities using machine learning algorithms which will become commonplace soon and will most likely feed a whole new topic for discussion.

What Risk Managers Say

Drone technology does not replace the risk manager, the underwriter, or the loss adjuster. It makes the individual players more effective and efficient in the processes they drive. It also plays a significant part in claims management and fraud prevention, and according to a 2019 Robotics Tomorrow article

'How Drones are Disrupting the Insurance Industry', drones can increase inspection efficiency by up to 85%[1].

According to Peter Olyott, CEO of Indwe (one of South Africa's largest independent brokers, offering personal, business and specialist risk and insurance advisory service), drones provide the entire insurance value chain with an innovative way to grow, to select risks more accurately and to add to the growing importance of data analytics in order to keep and/or create competitive advantages in an increasingly competitive and disrupted environment.

Industry commentators are also vocal about how significant the return on investment (ROI) of the use of drones in this industry can be. One of the best illustrations is a case in France, where an insurer used drone images to repudiate a €99m property claim caused by a fire that unknowingly started on a neighbouring property. The blog entitled 'Drone Map Saves Insurance Company €99,985,000', highlights the case study by Emilien Rose, founder of Dronotec, a start-up specialising in insurance drone inspections[2].

Drones also enable loss adjusters to get close to a roof, zoom in to questionable areas and analyse details to understand the cause and extent of the loss, all without disturbing the scene. In a mid-2019 analysis conducted by the Insurance Information Institute, fraud comprises about 10% of property and casualty insurance losses and loss adjustment expenses every year, which amounts to about $32 billion annually[3]. In the 2018 Deloitte InFocus report, commercial drones were estimated to help save the insurance industry nearly $7 billion per year through improved transaction processing and resource efficiency[4].

The use of drones in the insurance industry will continue to grow, with adoption in the commercial space increasing. There are already successful drone projects being delivered to large risk managers as described herein. However, there are also talks of using drones for rapid response to accident scenes, for example. That will most likely still take a while to implement successfully, although the idea is valid. Regulations still require permissions, and considerations of drone operations in controlled airspace, over backed up traffic on motor ways and safety of hovering over actual accident scenes with approaching medic helicopters, etc., are of paramount importance.

In conclusion, now that you have more insight into how the insurance sector is using drones to its advantage, it would not be amiss to assume that insurance companies and clients alike should insist on making drone technology part and parcel of the insurance echo system, for fear of being left behind by this fast-moving world, where data is king.

References

1. https://www.roboticstomorrow.com/article/2019/07/ how-drones-are-disrupting-the-insurance-industry/13938

2. https://medium.com/aerial-acuity/drone-map-saves-insurance-company-99-985-000-9c66094a097

3. https://www.roboticstomorrow.com/article/2019/07/ how-drones-are-disrupting-the-insurance-industry/13938

4. https://www2.deloitte.com/content/dam/Deloitte/us/ Documents/financial-services/us-fsi-infocus-drones-for-insurance.pdf

About Kim James

Kim spent over 20 years in the investment banking industry in South Africa, the United Kingdom, Hong Kong, and the United Arab Emirates. She has a master's degree in Human Resource Management from Middlesex University and is a Chartered HR Professional of the SA Board of People Practices. Kim is now fortunate enough to be using her global experience gained in  a highly regulated and structured industry, in the aviation field back in South Africa.

Kim is a Director of the SACAA-certified drone operation, UAV Aerial Works and the company's drone security brand, Drone Guards, as well as the regulatory Safety and Security post holder for UAV Aerial Works.

Aviation is her second career and passion, and among her latest achievements, a chapter in a co-authored Amazon #1 best seller, *Drone Professional 1*. Kim is also currently an Executive Committee member of CUAASA - the Commercial Unmanned Aircraft Association of Southern Africa.

Contacts

www.aerialworks.co.za

https://web.facebook.com/uavaerialworks

https://www.linkedin.com/in/kimjamesdrones

https://twitter.com/KimJamesDrones

kim@aerialworks.co.za

The Accidental Geek – Importance of Satellites

Ian Kiely

The night sky is soon to be awash with satellites, all sorts of shapes and sizes, whether we like it or not. How we harness their ingenuity is up to us.

When I decided to delve into the mysterious world of drones back in 2015, I had been a year recovering from injury, then illness and was just qualified as a project manager. I was in the food business for 20 years prior and quite tech adverse... I soon learned that while being a former technophobe made life more difficult, however it was not the end of the world, most people were only starting out on their drone journey. We were effectively making it up as we went along, regulation was being shaped and licensing was a new thing. Although not the first to take the Irish Aviation Authority, Remotely Piloted Aircraft Systems (RPAS) exam and flight test, I did manage to end up with licence document No. 000001 when they began printing them, therefore by default I am the No1 pilot :-) At least that is what I tell myself.

Like everyone starting out back then, the aim was to survive, operators were educating their potential clients, assuring people of safety and trying to convince the sceptics that we were onto something special, all while trying to find consistent paid work. Automated software, artificial intelligence and sensors had not caught up, most flights were manual, many facilities like proximity sensors that new pilots take for granted today had not been perfected or even dreamed of.

Before I took the test I was scribbling down ideas, how was I was going to make my millions? One such idea was aerial photography for the property market - not so original in hindsight. What dawned on me when I started drilling down and expanding ideas was *I am not thinking big enough*. I have had this revelation on several occasions since and each time the vision grows. It wasn't until mid-2018 that I fully understood the importance of satellites and how they would affect the future of drones and ultimately my career path.

Reliance On Satellites

Most drone professionals are aware that having good satellite connectivity provide: stable flight; the ability to hover with the confidence that the Unmanned aerial vehicle (UAV) is going to stay in place; and the likelihood that the loss of your drone is very slim.

Agriculture, data processing, search and rescue, nature conservation, mapping, construction and photography are all heavily reliant on satellite positioning. In simple terms this is achieved by timing the period it takes for a signal to reach the satellite and come back to the device. It is accurate to about eight meters so we use multiple satellites simultaneously to narrow that down to circa one meter.

Being in Ireland I am based on the edge of the European Union (EU). The European Space Agency (ESA) has been developing its own version of Global Positioning System (GPS) to assure satellite coverage to Europeans for generations to come. It consists of the Galileo – Global Navigation Satellite System

(GNSS) supported by the European Geostationary Navigation Overlay Service (EGNOS) (which effectively improves accuracy) and Copernicus – Earth Observation (EO). As an EU member state we are supported by services and funding to research and develop satellite based technologies including drones.

Here is a brief look at two relevant projects our team are currently working on: (November 2020).

GEONAV IoT

One of the EU support funds is known as Horizon 2020 (H2020). This mechanism for awarding grants is designed to foster collaboration between EU member states while connecting big industry with small and medium enterprises (SMEs) and encourage third level education to get involved as well.

Our consortium consists of two Polish companies: Chipcraft, Hertz Systems, Two French companies: Thales (leader), Telespazio and ourselves, Drone Consultants Ireland (DCI).

We are almost a year into collaboratively developing the next generation of satellite navigation chip. The initial plan was to provide services to elite sport and valuable asset tracking.

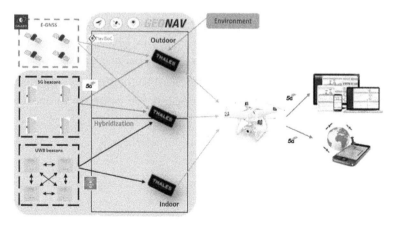

During the early stages of planning, when the DCI team were invited to join, we shared our vision for the future of drones and the potential autonomy of integrated Unmanned Aircraft System Traffic Management (UTM) and how that might work. With the arrival of delivery drones, the eagerly anticipated arrival of passenger drones and the expansion of commercial UAV services the skies will *need to be managed* with a holistic approach, a linked up system to make it all practical and safe even across borders.

GEONAV is a dual frequency chipset to improve performance and increase location accuracy both indoors and outdoors with a view to cross referencing the signal with 5G in built up areas or urban canyons. In basic terms, it has the capacity to correct itself against other satellite networks and 5G while using receivers in tight spaces (i.e., landing zones etc.,) to narrow down accuracy to mere centimeters. All of this information can be fed to one central system that can then be shared by all drone users and service providers.

I believe the safe integration of drones with Air Traffic Control and other drone users/operators is paramount for sustainable growth and the broader development of the industry. A variety of companies, educational institutions, civil aviation authorities and start-up businesses are developing UTM systems that they aspire to put forward as national or international solutions. Each organisation has their own approach and goals, some will be successful and others will fail, their central goal is safety and the capacity to *manage the skies*. At present there is no one method of craft communication being adopted. We hope to be one of the pieces of the puzzle.

"Jack in the Box" or JIB

This is the nick name we gave our passion project; we are currently developing this from our own pockets with a little help from the ESA Business Incubation Centre (ESABIC) and Enterprise Ireland (EI), the government business support network.

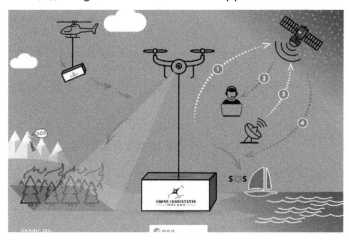

JIB is an aircraft deployable, tethered UAV system to help monitor and provide communications at wildfires and natural disasters for up to 500hrs with an aerial view in excess of 300sqKM.

A bespoke drone with very powerful day / night camera attached to a power up, data down tether are housed with a generator, fuel source and satellite communications system in a large robust box. This box is then launched by parachute from a fixed wing craft or delivered by helicopter to the point of emergency.

The drone, when remotely armed, will fly from the box to 100m above ground and attached to the tether (cable), provide visual data for at least 10KM in each direction. Ground crews, command and control, other aircraft and support responders can access the view of the camera through a dedicated search and rescue software, putting all stakeholders on the same page in real time with the capacity to communicate with each other.

Satellite Earth Observation is used to determine the drop site and the box itself will emit a satellite signal to determine its fixed location. This location can then be used as a reference point to establish where events are taking place through the camera. The visual data is streamed via satellite to a host of recipients and the UAV commands are issued back to the craft via satellite.

With this solution we are utilizing all the benefits the varying satellite constellations have to offer. We are not reliant on communications in remote locations or in areas of disaster where communications have the potential to be compromised.

Funding And The Space World

On top of the obvious benefits satellites bring to the table is the topic of money. Only in recent years have drone companies and peripheral industries begun attracting meaningful funding from private investors. Even more recently, the Venture Capital funds have come to the table reluctantly. Companies like Manna. Aero in Ireland, who are extremely advanced in their capacity to provide home delivery by drone (as of April 2020), are delivering medicines and groceries to peoples homes) have proved that this is possible and guess what, they rely on satellites all the time.

Space organisations such as the ESA, NASA and the UK Space Agency are making considerable funding available for research and development to encourage downstream uses of satellite services, the busier the satellites the more profitable they become and UAV demand is growing. I have attended space events all over the world and there is one thing that always amazes me. While we mere mortals are frowning over budgets in the tens or hundreds of thousands, their space budgets run into the billions. This is where the drone industry needs to be in a few short years. We need their support and they need our vision!

A Few Lessons Learned For The Beginner Starting Out

If you want to get started as a drone entrepreneur, do the usual stuff of setting up a business but try to pick one or two disciplines and stick to them. If other people are competing in this space, make sure you are offering better value. This does not mean cheaper! Know your worth and measure the toil you have invested. Charge accordingly. Offer a better level of service, manage client expectations and consistently provide a good quality deliverable.

It is very difficult to run a UAV business as an individual. Identify others with different sets of skills but with equal passion and build a team. Try not to be sucked in by idiots talking rubbish and openly flaunting regulations online (I am still grappling with this one).

Don't be afraid to ask for help / advice / a leg up and make sure to return the favour in equal measure. Do not fall into the trap of "do this job for us, it will be great exposure for you". If they really want you they will pay.

We are merely custodians of this new and exciting technology, young people now and those not born yet will be the ones to reap the greater benefits. They will also be the ones to perfect what we have started. Power supply will improve, noise levels will continue to decrease, safety and regulations will be addressed and the industry will keep evolving.

About Ian Kiely

Ian loves to work on mad projects and new ideas to collaborate with interesting and intelligent people….. as well as the practical stuff (to pay the bills).

Ian is co-founder and CEO of Drone Consultants Ireland and works on a variety of projects in addition to providing advice and support to a range of government entities, emergency responders and international industries.

The DCI team hosted Drone and Tech Expo Ireland for two years in Dublin and Ian is a guest MC for a number of other drone events across Europe.

Ian regularly features in all forms of media and is a well-known guest speaker, he also spends time working with kids to help ignite their passion for entrepreneurship through technology and mentors young (and old) drone pilots starting out.

Ian and his team won the Irish National Space Award 2018 and a European Space Award 2018 for satellite navigation.

Feel free to get in touch, if you don't hear back for a while don't worry he will get to you!

Contacts

ik@droneconsultantsireland.ie

https://www.linkedin.com/in/ian-kiely-a76444b3

Twitter: @skydronesian

The Use of Drone Technology For Informal Settlement Upgrading

Itumeleng Mokoena

I have always believed that if you want to profoundly change the course of history, you need to be intentional about it. It is not something that happens by chance or merely wishful thinking. Thus, it is my view that with the rapidly increasing emergence of drone technology and the various use cases it provides, it is imperative to ensure that the growing body of professionals in this space does not leave the less fortunate behind in this technology.

In recent years, there has been an exponential increase in the number of informal settlements (commonly referred to as slums) all over the world. According to the International Growth Centre, it is estimated that across the developing world, more than one billion people currently live in informal settlements with the expectation that by 2035, this number will have doubled[1]. For many African countries, governments have inherited ex-colonial policies that are ineffective in ensuring many ordinary citizens have access to adequate resources and housing facilities.

South Africa is no exception. Many of its citizens flock to suburban metros with the hope of finding greener pastures.

However, due to the lack of financial resources for adequate housing, many find themselves having to settle for shelter in areas with little to no infrastructure. Furthermore, the growth of these areas continues to overload already inadequate and overburdened infrastructure systems in the areas of waste collection, water and sanitation systems, roads, and increased air pollution, among others. In South Africa alone, it is estimated that there are more than three million individuals living in shacks in these informal settlements[2]. These shanty towns are a representation of the drastic socio-economic inequalities that exist because of the spatial segregation of the previous colonial administration.

How Do Drones Fit Into The Equation?

The applications of drones or remotely piloted aerial/aircraft systems (RPAS) has been on a steady increase in many industries. In comparison to manned or satellite imagery, drones can autonomously acquire high spatial and temporal resolution imagery at a more cost-effective rate.

© PartheniusAir

An image taken from mapping an informal settlement in Gauteng, South Africa

In South Africa, the Housing Development Agency (HDA) Act No. 23, 2008, is mandated to assist organs of State with the Implementation of the Upgrading of Informal Settlements. The National Upgrade Support Programme (NUSP) is one of the ways in which government aims to accelerate the implementation of these upgrades[3].

For the upgrade of these informal settlements to be effective, both the government and municipalities involved need to follow a community-based approach for the use of drones to ensure accuracy of the data and reliability. In situ slum upgrades implemented through participation of the community are widely considered global best practices in efforts to significantly improve the lives of at least 100 million shack dwellers[4].

Creating community-based programmes to teach both community members and their respective officials on how to accurately capture, process and report on the data obtained from drones can go a long way in ensuring that communities are able to sustain themselves beyond just taking images.

A community leadership organisation, called the Informal Settlement Network (ISN) engages government to improve the lives of the urban poor[5]. This is also key to ensuring that residents take responsibility for their own communities. Through the ISN, communities can participate actively in the upgrading of the informal settlements. This can be achieved through reblocking, a process in which the ground is levelled and taps, toilets and access to electricity is installed for each home.

To ensure that this process is done effectively, the ISN needs to have concise information about the settlement. The community further gets involved in the process of enumeration, whereby the number of structures, number of individuals staying in a particular household and the number the rooms each unit has are all counted.

This process of enumeration is generally done by walking on foot and can take several days. With the correct ground referencing systems and the use of drone technology, this process can be achieved in a much shorter space of time while providing an immeasurable amount of data that can be used by various key players such as civil engineers, town planners, disaster management teams, water, sanitation, and waste collection among others.

Flamingo Crescent – A Case Study

Flamingo Crescent, an informal settlement in Cape Town, was created in 2007 when the municipality relocated people living on streets and under bridges in Constantia, Wetton and Lansdowne to a vacant plot of municipal land in Lansdowne[6].

By 2012, the community consisted of 104 structures made of wood, plastic, cardboard, and aluminum. 405 people in this community shared 2 taps and 14 chemical toilets. Due to the lack of electricity, residents would survive by making fires in tin-drums as a source of heat and light. Furthermore, the lack of space presented major issues during summer seasons, when fires would occur, and presented flooding challenges in winter[7].

Through a long process of stakeholder engagement, the ISN, City of Cape Town Informal Settlement Department and the Community Organisation Resource Centre (CORC) were able to successfully reblock the informal settlement. This ensured that residents were afforded more space for each household, while also incorporating areas for early childhood development and recreation.

Having been exposed to the inequalities of being black and poor in South Africa, it is my desire to see an inclusive drone community that empowers those who need it the most and gives people a sense of direction and purpose. Through the education of drone technology, programmes such as the Flamingo Crescent can be improved to ensure that residents are equipped with skills that can benefit them beyond the reblocking process.

Working Towards An Inclusive Drone Culture

It is my view that one of the methods in which an inclusive drone culture can develop in informal settlements is by setting up programmes to teach kids in these communities about drone technology. This can be done through programmes such as the AeroBuddies[8] programme which teaches kids from ages as young as six about aeronautical concepts in a manner that makes it easy for them to enjoy learning about maths and science. In the case of Flamingo Crescent for example, one of the major challenges the community experienced was that they did not have proper facilities for childhood development.

A more practical example of the community participation using drones is a project that was carried out in Tanzania by the World Bank. The objective of the project was to create a digital terrain elevation model to generate reliable flood models and provide current, accurate, and detailed information for urban growth planning in the city[9]. This information was obtained by flying approximately 90 km of Dar-es-Salaam using multi rotor and fixed wing drones.

Following the flights, the Dar Ramani Huria participatory mapping exercise (which in Swahili means *to give open maps*) was carried out. This included training in cartography, field data collection with GPS and smartphones, and mapping in OpenStreetMap[10].

It is evident that while the use of drones for upgrading informal settlement is still in its infancy, creating programmes that are beneficial to these communities can go a long way in easing service delivery to citizens, while also ensuring that residents in these communities are given a sense of human dignity.

References

1. Collier, P., Glaesar, E., Venables, T. 2019. Informal settlements and housing markets. Policy Brief. Available at: https://www.theigc.org/wp-content/uploads/2019/01/informal-settlements-policy-brief.pdf Accessed: 15 November 2020

2. Housing Development Agency. 2013. Research Series. South Africa: Informal settlements status

3. Department Of Human Settlements. 2008. Housing Development Agency Act. No. 37899. Available at: https://www.gov.za/sites/default/files/gcis document/201409/37899rg10247gon610.pdf (Accessed: 20 November 2020)

4. Patel, K. 2013. A Successful Slum Upgrade in Durban: A Case of Formal Change and Informal Continuity. Habitat International. 40. 211-217. 10.1016/j.habitatint.2013.05.005.

5. https://www.sasdialliance.org.za/about/isn

6. https://www.sasdialliance.org.za/projects/flamingo-crescent

7. https://www.sasdialliance.org.za/projects/flamingo-crescent

8. Le Roux, K. 2017. Meet Joseph Phalwane and Jeff Cullis; owners of SA's best small businesses. Available at: http://www.702.co.za/articles/282669/meet-joseph-phalwane-and-jeff-cullis-owners-of-sa-s-best-small-businesses Accessed 29 November 2020

9. Vargas-Ramírez, N.; Paneque-Gálvez, J. The Global Emergence of Community Drones (2012–2017). Drones 2019, 3, 76.

10. Vargas-Ramírez, N.; Paneque-Gálvez, J. The Global Emergence of Community Drones (2012–2017). Drones 2019, 3, 76.

About Itumeleng Mokoena

Itumeleng defines herself as a dreamer, believer, pilot, artist, and lover. She is a licensed RPAS pilot and has completed over 200 flight hours within the commercial drone industry. Furthermore, she is a licensed RPAS instructor on both multirotor and fixed wing drones. She is also a certified RPAS Maintenance Technician. Outside of the aviation space, she holds a Non-Destructive  Testing Diploma and a BTech in Business Administration. She is also the Founder of Drone Pilot Network, a group which aims to assist people from previously disadvantaged backgrounds to get into the drone space in South Africa. Itumeleng is also the Operations Manager for Parthenius Air, a licensed ROC holder within the Republic of South Africa.

Contacts

https://www.linkedin.com/in/itumeleng-mokoena-10120683

itumeleng@parthenius-air.com

UAS Traffic Management (UTM): What Perspectives for the Future?

Filippo Tomasello

The rapid increase of drone's usage is before our eyes: more and more, these so-called Unmanned Aerial Vehicles (UAVs) are flocking the civil airspace and rapidly growing in popularity. Where do they come from?

Drones emerged for military purposes in the last decades of the 20th century. Starting from 2000, governmental non-military and civil uses started to emerge. Aviation regulatory authorities have been very cautious in allowing their gradual insertion into airspace. So, until 2015, operations of civil drones were essentially limited to Very Low Level (VLL), meaning at heights of less than 120 m (400 ft) or 150 m (500 ft) Above Ground Level (AGL) and in Visual Line-of-Sight (VLOS) from the remote pilot. This gradual approach allowed industry to initiate growth in this segment of aviation without compromising safety and societal acceptance.

Over time, the volume of activity of unmanned aerial vehicles has growing not only for recreational purposes but for a huge variety of aerial work applications. This growth poses several questions among which:

1. How to ensure enough safety and security of these activities without excessively burdening Small and Medium-sized Enterprises (SMEs) and overloading aviation authorities?

2. How to manage such high volumes of air traffic, as the current procedures are not suitable?

3. Which Communication, Navigation and Surveillance (CNS) technologies to use, since traditional aviation ground-based systems do not provide coverage at VLL over cities?

4. Which new services would be necessary and how to oversee them?

No consensus has been reached yet on the regulations and industry standards which should support the evolutionary growth of the market. The controversy starts already from the definitions: in USA the term 'UAS Traffic Management' is used, while in Europe European Union (EU) entities promote the use of the term 'U-Space'.

So, let's consider the current regulatory and standardisation developments, starting from the definitions.

What Is UTM?

According to the CORUS project[1], the EU has developed a vision called U-Space, which is *'a set of services designed to support safe, efficient and secure access to airspace for large numbers of drones.'* ICAO[2] instead used the term UTM, meaning *'a specific aspect of ATM which manages UAS operations safely, economically and efficiently through the provision of facilities and a seamless set of services in collaboration with all parties and involving airborne and ground-based functions.'* Conversely, no definition was proposed by the European Union Aviation Safety Agency (EASA) in the official Opinion[3] addressed to the European Commission (EC) in March 2020.

One may observe that, while the majority of experts in the global aviation community use the term 'UTM', in the EU that term was challenged, observing that at VLL there are not only 'unmanned', but also 'manned' aircraft (e.g. traditional helicopters in emergency services and with the pilot in the cockpit) and therefore any (air) traffic management concept should encompass both categories of airspace users. Nevertheless, also the term chosen by the EC (i.e. 'U-Space') as explained by CORUS still considers only drones.

Further work is hence necessary before achieving a definition acceptable by the vast majority of experts.

How Is UTM regulated?

Regulation of civil aviation started at international level in 1919 with the International Commission for Air Navigation Convention[4] and with the establishment of 'accident investigators' in Denmark and UK. In this occasion, the States promulgated a regulation containing detailed technical requirements and based on a 'prescriptive' approach. According to this approach, technical details are established by authority, often through acts having force of law and spread around the world with innumerable examples (some US Federal Aviation Regulations (FAR[5], the so called 'EU—OPS[6], Annex 10 to the Chicago Convention, etc.).

However, this prescriptive approach to regulation of civil aviation has at least three shortcomings:

- Complexity, as adoption at high level of organisations (e.g. the International Civil Aviation Organisation (ICAO) Council) or institutions (e.g. EC or even European Parliament) inevitably implies going through long procedures;
- Inability to respond rapidly to technological innovations;

- Rigidity, since technical details are 'frozen' in legally binding rules, which prevents applicants to propose new or alternative solutions.

As well as these shortcomings started to become prominent, there was a gradual change: Aviation Authorities around the world started speaking no longer about 'mandatory equipment', but more and more about 'Required Performance'. Finally, in 2002 the Legislator of the European Union (EU) established[7] EASA officially providing a solid legal basis for 'performance-based' safety regulation in the EU.

This new performance-based approach has been further implemented by two EC Regulations: the Commission Delegated Regulation 2019/945 and the Implementing Regulation 2019/947. The latter is particularly significant as it requires a risk assessment based on the Specific Operation Risk Assessment (SORA) for Specific operation. The SORA methodology, developed by the Joint Authorities for Rulemaking on Unmanned Systems (JARUS), leads to the identification of several risk mitigation measures to implement with a certain level of 'integrity' robustness and a certain level of 'assurance' robustness. To ensure integrity hence several consensus-based technical standards developed by Standard Development Organisations (SDOs) are necessary. In this perspective the Project AW-Drones plans to make available a single EU metastandard to guide industry and support the UTM.

There is not yet evidence that EC/EASA would apply the 'risk-based' approach to the regulation of the UTM services. However, readers may notice that CORUS[8] proposed around 20 different UTM services, while only about 1/3 are mentioned in the EASA Opinion[9] and proposed to be subject to certification by the aviation authorities. For instance, the UTM Communication Service (LCS), which is absolutely necessary to connect UAS operators, UTM users and UTM service providers (SPs) among them, is not mentioned in the EASA proposal, which can be justified assuming that UTM is 'safety-related', but not 'safety-critical' and hence not requiring direct oversight from the aviation authority.

According to Niall McCarthy[10], but based on data from ICAO, International Air Transport Association (IATA) and other authoritative sources, the number of fatalities due to accidents in Commercial Air Transport (CAT) around the entire world, was slightly above 1,000 in the year 2000 and since then it further decreased to few hundreds per year until end of 2019. Conversely, the World Health Organisation (WHO) reports[11] that mosquitoes are one of the deadliest animals in the world. Their ability to carry and spread disease to humans causes millions of deaths every year. In 2015, malaria alone caused 438,000 deaths. The general perception, hence, considers aviation is safe enough in comparison with other calamities. The consequence is that the resources assigned by the Government of the almost 200 Contracting States of ICAO are scarce and therefore, in several cases, respective Civil Aviation Authorities (CAAs) have growing difficulties in coping with volume and complicity of contemporary civil aviation.

To face this situation, and aware that it would not be feasible to request States to assign more resources to the CAAs, ICAO is promoting pooling resources at regional level through the Global Aviation Safety Oversight System (GASOS)[12]. However, this may not be enough and in fact, in its Legislative Proposal[13] of 2015, EC proposed that Qualified Entities (QEs) may be granted a privilege to issue, revoke, and suspend certificates on behalf of the Agency or national competent authority, so reducing the Level of Involvement (LoI) of the authorities for safety oversight.

The principle of taking advantage of accredited, competent and independent third parties, when high level of assurance robustness is required, is already embedded in SORA. But SORA is applicable to risk assessment of UAS operations, not directly to UTM services. I wonder: Why not apply the same principle also in the UTM context?

For example, requiring certification by authorities of providers of safety-critical UTM services and instead leaving for QEs the privilege of assessing safety-related SPs.

The terms 'safety critical' and 'safety related' are neither standard by ICAO, nor established by EU aviation safety Regulations. Several international standards exist covering 'safety related' systems: for example, ISO 26262 standard is applicable to the automotive industry and based on the general IEC 61508 standard, the use of a Safety Integrity Level (SIL). This standard is the basis a hazard is assessed considering the severity of its potential effects and the relative likelihood of the hazard to materialize. The determination of a SIL is the result of hazard identification and risk assessment, possibly using a risk matrix.

The SIL standardised by IEC and ISO comprises four levels of risk (or safety criticality), but it is substantially equivalent to using the risk matrix recommended by ICAO[14] which has five levels. Aerospace industry applies five levels of risk also to development of software.

However, even though the SIL/risk matrix approach classifies risks in five levels of growing safety criticality, all the standards and recommendations mentioned in this paragraph assume that there is one organisation (e.g. Design Organisation) taking the responsibility for the risk assessment.

Instead, in case of UTM one organisation may provide only safety related services, while other service providers may offer also safety critical services, and regulatory regimes may be different: e.g. safety critical services and related SPs certified by aviation authorities, while safety related could be verified through NBs or QEs. This would be perfectly consistent with the approach of SORA for UAS operations and more in general with risk-based regulation, reducing the level of involvement of authorities, while still ensuring sufficient protection of society.

So far there is no evidence of the regulatory aviation authorities going in this direction for UTM services, but one may notice:

- ICAO in paragraph 2.2.2 its Annex 3 [15] mandates that each Contracting State shall ensure that the designated Meteorological (MET) SPs establishes and implements a properly organised quality system. However, this provision does not require certification by State (or CAA) being followed by Recommendation 2.2.3 suggesting that the quality system should be in conformity with the ISO 9000 series of quality assurance standards and should be certified by an approved organisation (i.e. NB or QE using the terminology of this article);

- Equal provisions are established in paragraph 3.6.1 and Recommendation 3.6.2 of ICAO Annex 15 [16] with reference to SPs of Aeronautical Information Service (AIS).

- In its Opinion [17], EASA listed only 8 U-Space (UTM) services, omitting the Communication (COM) service, which could perhaps be interpreted that this service was considered by EASA safety related, but not safety critical;

- The list of services identified by CORUS is much longer than the one from EASA and it would be disproportionate to regulate all of them through certification by the aviation authorities.

To pursue risk-based regulation even for UTM services and related SPs, it would be necessary to first establish a clear distinction between safety related and safety critical services. The author of this article has hence proposed to WG/4 of ISO TC/20 SC/6 to introduce in ISO 23629-12 the draft definitions presented in Table 1:

Term	Definition
Safety critical UTM service	UTM service providing functions that, if lost or degraded, or as a result of incorrect or inadvertent operation, would result in catastrophic consequences
Safety related UTM service	UTM service providing functions that, if lost or degraded, or as a result of incorrect or inadvertent operation, would result in catastrophic consequences

Possible adoption of these (or similar) differential definitions by ISO would of course not dictate any specific regulatory regime, since this is obviously a prerogative of the competent authorities and not of ISO.

But in the opinion of the author of this article, consensus-based definitions adopted by ISO, would facilitate discussion in regulatory authority towards a possible performance-based and risk-based regulation of UTM services.

References

1. CORUS, U-Space Concept of Operations (CONOPS), Bruxelles (EU), 4 September 2019. https://www.eurocontrol.int/project/concept-operations-european-utm-systems

2. ICAO, Unmanned Aircraft Systems Traffic Management (UTM) – A Common Framework with Core Principles for Global Harmonization, Edition 2, Montreal (CAN). https://www.icao.int/safety/UA/Documents/UTM-Framework%20Edition%202.pdf

3. EASA, High-level regulatory framework for the U-space, Opinion No 01/2020, Cologne (EU), 13 March 2020. https://www.easa.europa.eu/document-library/opinions/opinion-012020

4. Paris Convention, Convention Relating to the Regulation of Aerial Navigation, Versailles (France), 13 October 1919. https://untermportal.un.org/unterm/Display/record/UNHQ/Convention_for_the_Regulation_of_Aerial_Navigation/E8A725A703847FAC852569FA00002BF7

5. FAA website https://www.faa.gov/regulations_policies/faa_regulations/

6. Commission Regulation (EC) No 859/2008 of 20 August 2008 amending Council Regulation (EEC) No 3922/91 as regards common technical requirements and administrative procedures applicable to commercial transportation by aeroplane, Bruxelles (EU), 20 August 2008. https://eur-lex.europa.eu/LexUriServ/LexUriServ.do?uri=OJ:L:2008:254:0001:0238:En:PDF

7. EU, Regulation (EC) No 1592/2002 of the European Parliament and of the Council of 15 July 2002 on common rules in the field of civil aviation and establishing a European Aviation Safety Agency.

8. CORUS, U-Space Concept of Operations (CONOPS)

9. Paris Convention, Convention Relating to the Regulation of Aerial Navigation, Op. cit.

10. Niall McCarthy, 2019 Was A Safe Year For Air Travel Despite MAX Woes, 2 January 2020. https://www.statista.com/chart/12393/2017-wasWHO web site https://www.who.int/neglected_diseases/vector_ecology/mosquito-borne-diseases/en

11. WHO web site https://www.who.int/neglected_diseases/vector_ecology/mosquito-borne-diseases/en/

12. ICAO, GASOS website https://www.icao.int/safety/gasos/Pages/default.aspx

13. EC, Proposal for a Regulation of the European Parliament and of the Council on common rules in the field of civil aviation and establishing a European Union Aviation Safety Agency, and repealing Regulation (EC) No 216/2008 of the European Parliament and of the Council, COM/2015/0613 final, Bruxelles (EU), 7 December 2015. https://eur-lex.europa.eu/legal-content/EN/TXT/?qid=1587292166566&uri=CELEX:52015PC0613

14. ICAO, Safety Management Manual, Doc 9859, 4th edition, Montreal, 2018.

15. ICAO, Annex 3 to the Chicago Convention, Meteorological Service for International Air Navigation, 20th edition including amendment 78, Montreal, 2018.

16. ICAO, Annex 15 to the Chicago Convention, Aeronautical Information Service, 16th edition including amendment 40, Montreal, 2018.

17. EASA, High-level regulatory framework for the U-space, Op. cit.

About Filippo Tomasello

Filippo Tomasello was flight test engineer in Italian Air Force until 1984. Subsequently, responsible in ENAV for R&D and modernisation projects. Manager for Northern Europe in EUROCONTROL since 2000. From 2005 at European Commission on extension of EASA remit to ATM/ANS and aerodromes. In EASA from 2007 to Jan 2015, Tomasello developed rules on ATM, aerodromes, flight operations, flight crew licensing and initial airworthiness, including related impact assessments. Since 2008 he was focal point for rulemaking on Unmanned Aircraft. Member or chair of several ICAO bodies. Tomasello was consultant of ICAO for the GASOS Manual (2017-20). In JARUS, he was rapporteur of WG/2. Foreign Expert at *http://ev.buaa.edu.cn/* from 2017 to 2019.

Now Professor of aviation safety at the University Giustino Fortunato. In January 2015, he founded EuroUSC Italia, where now he is Senior Partner. He also supports the Qatar participation to JARUS and, in ICAO, is member of the Space "Learning Group" and observer in the RPAS Panel. Member of the EASA Expert Group on UAS certified category. Member of Eurocae WG 105 (UAS) on behalf of University Giustino Fortunato and of ISO TC/20 SC/16 on behalf of Italy (UNI).

Contacts

filippo.tomasello@eurousc-italia.it

linkedin.com/in/filippo-tomasello-a96490b

https://twitter.com/euro_uscit_FTom

Affiliations

https://www.eurousc-italia.it/en

https://www.unifortunato.eu

It Takes A Team To Get Airborne

Gift Kgadima

As I take a deep breath, I buckle up, strapping myself into my seat. The windsock in the distance moves slightly, indicating a light and variable gust of wind. My instructor walks up to me assisting with strapping me in securely. He then says:

"It's time, just relax and follow procedures through."

I try to maintain composure, and with a straight face, nod in agreement.

Seated in a glider, I am 30 seconds away from my first ever solo flight. I close the canopy, and call on the radio, *Take up slack. Take up slack* indicating to the aerotow aircraft in front of me that I am ready for takeoff. The pilot in the aircraft that will be towing me in the glider calls on the radio that he is rolling on runway 02.

"Brits Traffic, this is Charlie Uniform Echo, rolling runway 02 for a glider tow."

As the glider begins to roll on the runway, I realise that there is no turning back. I take another deep breath and keep my eyes on the aerotow aircraft ahead of me. With the airspeed increasing, my nerves begin to calm down, and within a few seconds I pull back on the control stick with the glider getting airborne. We take off and I release from the aerotow at 2,000 feet Above Ground Level. As I break away in-formation from the aerotow aircraft, I shout, *Yebo!* barely able to contain my excitement. I did it - my first solo takeoff. After 30 minutes of flying, I land safely and receive congratulations from my instructor, much to his relief.

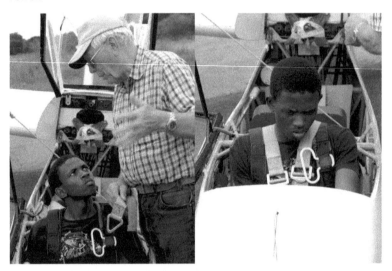

That 30 minute flight took months and months of preparation and working closely with a team of great instructors. I realized there and then, the significant role a team plays in the success of any operations. I have since adopted a team/ people centric approach to drone operations, because drone operations are similar to gliding: a group of people come together working towards a common goal, to ensure a safe flight.

As a drone professional, I work with a team and interact with people outside my team; working together collectively towards a common goal- a goal of a safe drone flight. Granted, drones may be machines, it is the people, however, who complete the operations.

Depth In DIVERSITY

In South Africa, we have various ethnicities and people coming from different backgrounds. This is also the case in the global community. The aviation industry in South Africa doesn't have enough representation of people of colour, more so women. The commercial drone industry, young as it is, could be the leader in building a diverse industry. I truly believe that the drone industry is in a position to achieve what no other aviation sector can- it can dismantle the previous barriers that prohibited Diversity.

The commercial drone industry is still at its teething phase and as such, the majority of industry players are people who are/ were professionals in other industries and sectors of the economy. The industry is a culmination of different expertise and different people coming together to build the industry. When you build a team that will operate/ work with you, it is imperative to include diversity in your expansion strategy. I have learnt that diversity brings a lot of depth to drone operations when you bring people from different backgrounds to work together towards a common goal- we all have something to bring to the table.

I worked with a great friend of mine in drone anti-poaching operations around Southern Africa, and being in the same age group did not make us a great team - it was our willingness to embrace our diversity that made us a great team.

I was raised in a township situated in Johannesburg and he was raised in Cape Town suburbia, but both our experiences of the world was what navigated us in sometimes challenging situations.

Our bond became exceptional because we understood each other's points of view. Our anti-poaching operations in Zimbabwe brought us a myriad of challenges and thankfully we were able to overcome them. Being South African, we had to allow ourselves to learn, immerse ourselves with the local culture and understand their way of thinking. We had to break all the cultural barriers in order for us to work meaningfully with Zimbabwean rangers and authorities. The operation wouldn't have been successful if, when establishing operations in a foreign country, it we had not included diversity.

That said, I really encourage all those who are in the drone industry, along with those who wish to be part of it, to really have an open mind; respect people, and see them for who they are. Allow diversity to be the fuel to growing this industry together. Looking at the aviation sector as a whole, we can all agree that there is a need for transformation; the diversity conversation must be had. The drone industry can really pave a way for this by being the industry that adopts a different complexion, which eliminates the necessity for any form of transformation in the future. This is possible- only if we all work together.

Inclusivity Must Not Be Exclusive

Inclusion is a different concept from diversity. It pertains to how you make the team members feel. Drone operations may be centered around the pilot, whose duty is to ensure that the unmanned aircraft vehicle is flown safely to meet the set objectives, but outside of that, he/she is also responsible for the culture of inclusivity that is fostered on site. Company management is faced with the responsibility of making sure that all role players feel fully part of the team.

I was recently part of a bridge inspection where I was the pilot in command for the operations. There were various parties that made up the operational team with one objective: to capture the correct data needed by the bridge engineer. The unmanned aerial vehicle that was utilized was a DJI drone that had been modified with Lidar (Light Detection and Ranging) hardware which would aid in the operations. Given that we were flying underneath a bridge, the unmanned aerial vehicle was deprived of GPS signal (which helps the drone fly with precise positioning). The minimal to no GPS signal meant that the unmanned aerial vehicle would be more challenging to fly, what with wind and gusts blowing around the bridge. The Lidar hardware was meant to enable the drone to map its surrounding in real time and use that information for its positioning.

The team that was in charge of putting the hardware together played a more important role than me, and naturally, I had to make them feel just as important to the operations, because often, the pilot is always praised at the expense of other team members. Highlighting their importance made it possible for us to successfully complete the task- as a team.

Creating that space where everyone felt as though they can contribute made it possible to tackle issues encountered collectively.

The Flight Begins With Collaboration

For most drone operations, with the exception of drone security and surveillance operations, flying is a fraction of the time relative to an operation. Of course the objective might be to capture the required data based on the scope; however, the planning for the execution requires preparatory work. Once on site, the flight will most likely take minutes and you'll have the required data. The planning leading up to those few minutes, is vital to the success of the flight. In preparation for a flight, a lot of collaboration from various departments and internal and external individuals will be required. This requires people skills, and for one to be comfortable engaging with other people. Collaboration is important, and it becomes easier to execute when engagements have a level of comfort.

COMMUNICATION

In our younger years, my friends and I used to play a game called Broken Telephone. One friend would begin by whispering something into another's ear, who would then pass it on to another, and the chain would continue until all those playing had whispered in each other's ears. Most times, the message would end up being distorted. In an operational scenario, broken communication could be detrimental. As a leader in drone operations, effective communication with your team members is necessary to avoid any grey areas or uncertainties. With a clearly communicated mandate, the team knows what is expected of them and what the objectives are; their roles and responsibilities are communicated so every team member knows what their exact role will be in the operations to be conducted. On site communication is just as important- the pilot in command must brief everyone involved in the operations and set the operational guidelines. This pre-flight briefing comes in handy in case of emergency; it's always in unexpected situations that the team's experience is tested and a briefing will guide how the emergency is handled, mitigating risk.

It has been seldom that I have been on site and never encountered any technical issue or an unexpected curve ball. Those instances are well handled when you open the floor to the team on site. Allow everyone the opportunity to suggest a solution to the issue at hand. Some team leaders are quick to shut down any suggestions that other members may propose to assist in finding a solution. As a pilot in command, I always listen to suggestions and input from the other team members. By systematically trying the suggestions given, you encourage the other team members to also think of solutions to the problem at hand. This may sometimes require patience as some suggestions could sound ridiculous to you. That suggestion may sound ridiculous, but some people are not very articulate and so, you could lose their point. That does not mean you must not try to implement their suggestion. In some instances, I found that it was the team member who was not able to articulate the solution effectively that solved the problem. Much of communication is you listening and not always being quick to talk over others. Communicate, implement and re-iterate, but never shut anyone out. That platform of communication enables the team to collectively get the operations back on schedule much quicker.

TRUST: The Glue That Holds it All Together

You cannot learn everything by yourself. None of us is as smart as all of us. When you are involved in drone operations, trust the expertise that everyone brings to the team. Trust serves as a means to delegate effectively without having to question your fellow team member.

When you are intentional about Diversity and Inclusivity, you are creating an environment where people can be authentic. When you allow the team members to be authentic and true to themselves, trusting them becomes easier.

When people hold back and aren't true to who they are, it creates a trust barrier. Let authenticity thrive, breaking down any layers which block trust.

In as much as I advocate for trust, trust in its nature opens you up to being vulnerable. Accountability will serve as a means of making sure that the trust relationship is not easily violated. Trust will need more of a long term approach, so start with a measure approach by delegating tasks to team members based on what they are able to do. Give the team member you are delegating, enough resources to complete the task at hand. Once he/she has successfully completed the task, then you can trust the individual with slightly more demanding tasks. Do this over and over again till you are comfortable with your trust level, given the execution of the team member.

If you are looking to get involved in drone operations or currently in the industry looking to improve your operations, I hope that what I have shared will be just the information required helping you reach greater heights.

About Gift Kgadima

Gift Kgadima has been privileged to be involved in the aviation industry from a young age, when he initially learnt to fly and become a glider pilot at sixteen years of age. In 2018, Gift established a company called Nafasi Za Angani *Nafasi*, where he is the Chief Executive Officer and co-founder. Nafasi is a world class data collection, processing and analytics company that uses drone technology along with other 3D scanners to provide innovative business solutions. Their focus area is the built environment industry assisting AEC professionals incorporate digital data in their workflows.

Gift serves on the board of Wonders of Aviation, a non-profit organisation that uses flight to engender a culture of long life learning. Gift Serves as vice chairman at Wonders of Aviation. Gift also serves on and the council of the Royal Aeronautical Society of South Africa, a fully-fledged division of the Royal Aeronautical Society.

Contacts

gift.k@nafasi.co.za

www.nafasi-za.com

www.linkedin.com/in/gift-kgadima

www.linkedin.com/company/nafasi-africa

Drone Manufacturing Journey – You Dream It, We Build It!

Queen Ndlovu

How It All Started

"Oops! Are you an aeronautical or an industrial engineer by profession? Whaaaat! A drone factory... Capital intensive... Who is going to fund you? Unions... Did you really think through this? Importing is cheaper... Why the trouble? You cannot beat the Chinese pricing and manufacturing capability... Why bother?"

Everyday, I am confronted with these remarks whenever I am interacting with various stakeholders for our drone manufacturing start-up. I will respond that I am not an engineer by profession, but I am certainly a Technopreneur. I tell them that I partner with design and systems engineers to commercialize the innovation that we intend to patent and manufacture. Therefore, as a serial entrepreneur I surround myself with technical individuals to identify and exploit gaps in the market, emerging tends or emerging industries.

Manufacturing is capital-intensive but should not be the reason why we do not pursue manufacturing in Emerging African Economies (EAEs). Granted, it is expensive, but we aspire to build a profitable lean and a smart global drone factory here in Africa. South Africa drone startups are aiming to hit it big globally — in both developing and emerging markets... [1]. This statement keeps me motivated about the commercial markets chosen by QP Drone Tech (QP).

Our journey started in 2017, when I took a sabbatical and returned to school to pursue my business studies focussing on high-tech. As a serial entrepreneur for more than two decades, I have founded and co-founded several small ventures. Though successful, I decided to become a futurist and search for innovative businesses with a high entrepreneurial orientation. *The business school might expose one to the businesses of the future,* I thought.

I enrolled in a Masters Degree of Entrepreneurship and New Venture Creation Degree at Witwatersrand (Wits) Business School. High Growth and Technology Entrepreneurship (Technopreneurship) and Global Entrepreneurship were the two modules that inspired me most. Coincidentally, one of the course coordinators Dr. Murimbika continuously challenged us on the importance of becoming the real game changers beyond one's immediate environment. I was exposed to the concept of born-global start-up ventures. I subsequently decided to become a born global, and create a global startup registered both in South Africa and abroad.

Having completed the course work and waiting for the outcome of the research proposal, I was then accepted at the Peking Business School in Shenzhen, China. I spent six months learning about Chinese business culture, cross-borders enterprises; learned Mandarin; and studied the drone industry in China.

This is where I also met one of my fellow Directors, Qin Longjun, who had just started his PhD in drones. We later attracted other Directors and partners to complement the team, but my first encounter with Qin was when he flew a drone on campus. We started our own founders garage story spending many long hours, sometimes into the early hours of the morning in his laboratory. We travelled to other provinces, such as Beijing, to explore different drone applications and Research and Development capabilities.

Eventually, a business decision was made to manufacture fixed wing drones.

We started QP Drone Tech in Shenzhen followed proudly by QP Drone Tech in South Africa. I applied what I had learned about the established drone industry in China but quickly realized that there is so much more to learn about the emerging drone industry, here at home.

My first encounter with Qin and the drone he was flying at the campus in Peking campus, China.

Back to Umzansi, South Africa - Back to Reality

"Formal education will make you a living, self-education will make you a fortune."[2]

According to the South African Additive Manufacturing Strategy[3], one of the focus areas for the South was the integrated product development, process, and production system design to speed up production time. Additive Manufacturing (AM) is a key technology that drives this objective especially within the aerospace industry.

With that in mind, I attended numerous drone conferences, familiarizing myself with the regulations, and sourcing out who the real players are and engaging with critical stakeholders in the industry such as CSIR, AMSCOR and DENEL.

QP has focused on security and surveillance applications. We have sought potential partnerships with established critical stakeholders with massive infrastructure and wealth of knowledge at their disposal.

I conducted extensive literature reviews on the drone industry in South Africa confirming that *Agriculture, surveillance and security are emerging growth points for the drone industry to adopt should advances in technology persist and more complex operations be approved by the SACAA* (State of Drone Report in South Africa, 2018)[4].

While clear on our value proposition, navigating a drone startup has been an emotional roller coaster ride.

Pre-seed, seed funding from family, friends, and fans - or any other form of angel funding - is a prerequisite for success in this industry. I come from a consulting background where you do not require as much investment prior to launching a successful business. But I discovered bootstrapping QP was not a sustainable model.

Therefore, I approached the Innovation Hub. Subsequently, I joined a Drone Accelerator programme offered by Mzansi Aerospace. I also attended Startup Cycle, spearheaded by Mr. Sandras Phiri. In total, I have now participated in three accelerator programmes. The Innovation Hub sponsored the launch of our high fidelity Minimal Viable Product (MVP). The event enabled us to demonstrate our MVP, and we received valuable insights from industry experts; and attracted potential clients and investment.

The Startup Cycle specifically enabled me to sharpen my pitching skills. Each week we had to pitch to a panel of mentors and potential investors. As the CEO and Co-Founder of QP Drone, I have now had to make numerous presentations which have left me drained and despondent, as well as excited and kindled. I've discovered that the most critical person to pitch to is yourself. Pitching often has become like a rejection vaccine: the more you pitch the less fear you have, which ultimately leads to a win.

Whether its ten minutes or one minute, pitching for funding for a manufacturing innovation entity has been a challenge but being chosen as one of the Top Finalist for Women in Tech by South African Innovation Summit (2020) was a sobering result. And a nomination to participate in London Tech week has been truly phenomenal.

I also discovered various opportunities offered via government schemes and grants i.e., Department of Trade and Industry, SEDA. While eager to assist tech start-ups the administration and turnaround times tends to be cumbersome and slow. Commercial drone technology is a new and an emerging industry, that is heavily-regulated with entry barriers.

Combining manufacturing and high tech makes it an even tougher challenge.

Twigging It A Bit -Pivoting

*"The longer you're are not taking action
the more money you're losing."*[4]

The challenge for QP has been gaining customers and financial traction for the manufacturing model. The initial business model was to import drones from China, assemble them in South Africa and later progress to the global greenfield.

We have since refined our revenue model with a pivot to offer consulting services across all industries to deliver end-to-end solutions through strategic partnerships with operations to fly commercially. This does not mean that we have abandoned our manufacturing dream. It means QP remains sustainable as we raise funds to build our smart lean drone factory.

The firm is already capitalizing on the wealth of knowledge acquired over the past 20 months. And we are starting to see that the decision to pivot is beginning to pay off. At the time of writing, we are in discussions with two multinational brands that have demonstrated a keen interest in joining forces with QP.

This has been a long journey with a steep learning curve, however, I cannot wait for the next edition of *Drone Professional,* hopefully to share our success.

References

1. Trimm. S. (Editor) (2019), 'SA Drone Startups, Companies Look Overseas To Shore Up Business', Ventureburn, (2019) https://ventureburn.com/2019/09/sa-drone-companies-look-to-foreign-shores/, accessed 15 November 2020

2. Henry. M. (2015) Jim Rohn Self education will make you a fortune, [online video], https://youtu.be/RVCNoTq3DcY

3. de Beer. D., du Preez. W., Greyling. H., Prinsloo. F., Sciammarella. F., Trollip. N., Vermeulen. M., Wohlers. T. (2016). A South African Additive Manufacturing Strategy, CSIR Publications

4. https://rocketmine.com/state-of-drone-report-2018

5. Wilkerson. C (2011). The Barefoot Executive: The Ultimate Guide for Being Your Own Boss and Achieving Financial Freedom. HarperCollins Leadership

About Queen Ndlovu

Ms Ndlovu is a serial entrepreneur and the CEO and Co-Founder of QP Drone Tech. Over 23 years, Ms Ndlovu founded and co-founded various Artisan Colleges, a management consultancy, and a dry cleaning and laundry business and is a partner in maritime and an energy business.

Ms Ndlovu has a Masters degree in Entrepreneurship and New Venture Creation from Wits business school; and a Post Masters qualification from Peking Business School, China.

A keynote speaker at various institutions such as Oprah School of Girls and a Guest Lecturer at various Business Schools, she is currently the Chairperson for the Academic Advisory Board: Entrepreneurship Department at Tshwane University of Technology. She is a pitching finalist in the South African Tech Innovation Summit (2020).

She is a Deputy President of African Alliance of YMCAs to spearhead social enterprise as to drive social innovation, social impact, and sustainability amongst the youth.

Contacts

https://www.linkedin.com/in/queen-ndlovu-3074819

https://www.linkedin.com/company/qpdronetech

https://www.qpdronetech.co.za

queen@qpdronetech.co.za

UTM: A Modern Day Wright Brothers Moment

Dean Polley

I have always been fascinated by the story of the Wright Brothers and their perseverance to master powered and controlled flight. Throughout history, there have been countless records demonstrating man's fascination with flight, with stories dating back many centuries. I'm sure most of us are familiar with the story in Greek mythology with the legend of Daedalus and Icarus, the father and son who created wings by combining feathers and wax.

Leonardo Da Vinci was fascinated with the possibility of human mechanical flight having produced more than 35,000 words and 500 sketches dealing with flying machines, the nature of air, and bird flight.

When Orville and Wilbur Wright recorded their first successful powered and controlled flight on the 17th of December 1903, that event would set a new standard for aviation and would effectively be the birth of modern day aviation. What fascinates me about their story is that it took many years of trial and error to eventually achieve their objective. That single event was not an immediate catalyst for the adoption of commercial aviation however, as one would have imagined. A further six years would transpire before they would finally convince their first client, the US military, to sign the first contract to manufacture their flying machine.

From that defining moment, the adoption of commercial aviation increased dramatically and by 1914 the world's first scheduled passenger air service had begun. The 1920s and 1930s were a time of explosive growth in civil aviation. Revolutionary aircraft designs helped make air travel more accessible and comfortable for the public. Intercontinental travel times were reduced from weeks and months to days and hours.

1944 was a key moment in aviation history, with the establishment of the Convention on International Civil Aviation, or better known as the Chicago Convention. The agency's goal was to standardise the efficiency, safety and consistency of all civil flights. With an increase in global air travel, air safety became a priority and air traffic control became increasingly challenging.

Air Traffic Control And Radar

The 1950s saw the introduction of radar for controlling the approach of aircraft at airports. Radar was able to "see" aircraft through the reflected radio signals bouncing off the aircraft surface. Transponders were later introduced which allowed an aircraft to communicate its position with air traffic control. In simplistic terms, a ground based radar system would continuously send out signals in a reserved frequency spectrum (1030Mhz) and the onboard transponder would receive the signal and respond with a confirmation signal (1090Mhz).

The first transponders operated in what was termed Mode A, which was simply a transmission of an identification code, known as a "squawk code". This 4-digit squawk code would be provided to the aircraft pilot by an air traffic controller by way of radio communication. The pilot would then key in this squawk code and with each radar interrogation signal received, the transponder would transmit the squawk code back to air traffic control, thereby allowing them to locate the aircraft in airspace.

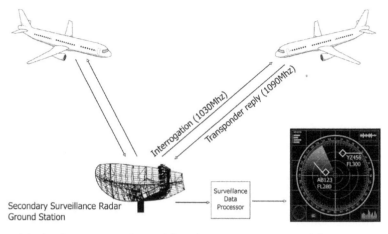

Secondary Surveillance Radar
Ground Station

Mode C transponders either have an integrated barometer or connect to an external barometer and together with the squawk code, the aircraft's pressure altitude is also transmitted, providing that added information to air traffic control.

Another mode called Mode S was designed to help avoiding over interrogation of the transponder, i.e., having too many radars in busy areas, and to allow automatic collision avoidance. Mode S transponders are compatible with Mode A and Mode C Secondary Surveillance Radar (SSR) systems, and this is the type of transponder that is used for TCAS (Traffic Collision Avoidance System) or ACAS II (Airborne Collision Avoidance System) functions.

Enter ADS-B: See And Be Seen

The next and latest generation of aircraft surveillance technology is ADS-B (Automatic Dependent Surveillance – Broadcast). ADS-B was developed to transmit aircraft position, heading and velocity in three dimensions to other aircraft via an air-to-air datalink and to ground stations via an air-to-ground datalink (ADS-B Out). The primary difference with this technology is that ADS-B does not require a radar interrogation signal in order to transmit a response, the transponder transmits continuously, or broadcasts its position continuously. Any other aircraft and ground stations can receive these broadcasted signals and can therefore calculate and display relative range and bearing (ADS-B In). In addition, data gathered from ADS-B Out equipped aircraft are fed to Air Traffic Control. Like TCAS, ADS-B requires ALL aircraft be equipped in order to receive full benefit from the system. If one aircraft lacks a Mode C transponder, that aircraft is invisible to the TCAS equipped aircraft. Likewise with ADS-B, if an aircraft is not broadcasting its location in airspace, the aircraft with ADS-B In won't "see" them. Therefore, SSR installations must continue to be operated in the airspace until ALL aircraft have ADS-B Out capabilities. The justification for legal mandates to "motivate" the aviation industry and consumers to equip needs to be driven by regulators.

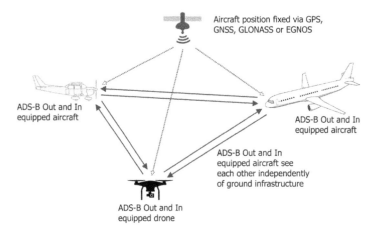

Aircraft position fixed via GPS, GNSS, GLONASS or EGNOS

ADS-B Out and In equipped aircraft

ADS-B Out and In equipped aircraft

ADS-B Out and In equipped aircraft see each other independently of ground infrastructure

ADS-B Out and In equipped drone

The advent of ADS-B transponders will most likely prove to be the key enabler for the standardisation and implementation of a global UTM (Unmanned Traffic Management) system.

UTM - Unmanned Traffic Management

We stand on the brink of another exciting point in the history of aviation and the skies are busier than ever. The past decade has seen an exponential increase in the use of commercial unmanned aircraft, more commonly known as drones. The use of drones has started to permeate our everyday lives with a multitude of applications, ranging from aerial survey and mapping, security and surveillance, photography and filming to vital infrastructure and hazardous environment inspections, to name a few.

But there is another change on the horizon. An entirely new category of airspace user is on the rise, with self- and remotely-piloted aircraft developing rapidly. Soon, autonomous aircraft will be transporting people and goods all around the world. As we speak, companies like Airbus, Boeing, Hyundai and Uber are developing and actively testing this new mode of human transport, termed UAM (Urban Air Mobility).

So what is UTM? Today, aircraft are guided around the skies by air traffic controllers. Each controller is responsible for a sector, keeping aircraft safe by talking directly with pilots using radio communications. Estimates show that the growth of commercial air traffic is already exceeding the capacity of a human-centered system and that is only for human-piloted flights. The expected growth of unmanned and self-piloted operations will increase traffic by several orders of magnitude.

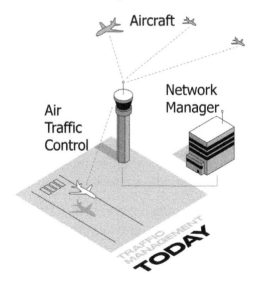

To handle this dramatic growth, air traffic management must shift to a more scalable model, a digital system that can monitor and manage this increased activity. That system is what we call Unmanned Traffic Management, or UTM.

UTM is not a single, central system that mandates one way of operating for everything. Instead, it is a framework. It is a networked collection of services that join together and understand each other, based on common rules.

UTM is built to enable future applications. The challenge is designing a system that can remain relevant as technology progresses and market needs mature without knowing what that future will look like. Rather than relying on centralised control, UTM frameworks around the world use the principle of distributed authority. This opens up the system to more service providers, who can adapt as the market evolves and needs change.

Decentralization privatises the cost of serving and adapting to market needs, while government regulators remain key for ensuring that safety, access, and equity are maintained. In reality, this means aircraft are no longer forced to talk only to a single entity, such as an assigned air traffic controller. Instead, aircraft can communicate freely with their service providers of choice, who are held to relevant safety, security, and performance standards by the authorities and coordinate with the rest of the network to make efficient decisions based on specific flight objectives.

Human air traffic controllers, meanwhile, will become airspace managers, focused on oversight, safety, and security. UTM allows the same foundation to serve different needs in different geographies at different times.

Regulators can adapt requirements to match their local needs, and operators can select the providers they need to complete their missions. Providers can create, update and deploy their own services quickly. One operator can choose to build, certify and supply its own services, while another may find the same services in a marketplace. Providers will be responsible for coordinating with each other.

For unmanned applications to thrive, many stakeholders will need to come together to advance their respective domains. Advances can be accomplished in phases, with each phase dependent on the previous ones. As UTM shows positive results, there may be technology sharing or increased integration with traditional Air Traffic Management.

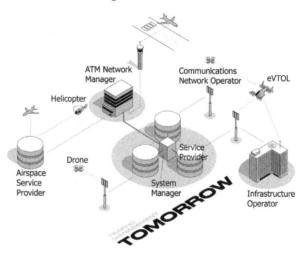

In Conclusion

The Wright Brothers couldn't possibly have imagined what the spin-offs of their invention would bring to the world. Similarly, I don't think that many ordinary people at that time could have imagined what air travel would be like in fifty to a hundred years time.

Considering the modern day rapid rate of technological advancements, the development and testing of autonomous people carrying aircraft, the existence of the next phase of miniaturised electronic conspicuity devices such as ADS-B transponders and the push towards a global standard in UTM systems, the concept of hailing an air taxi using your Uber app on a smartphone to fly you from one SkyPort to another over a crowded city, is a matter of a few decades away, if not sooner.

I contemplate where we are today and what the visions and plans are for an aviation future that is so tangible, one can virtually see it rather than imagine it. I can't help but wonder what it must have been like back in 1903 when Orville and Wilbur Wright were working on their dream of manned flight and what their visions were for the future. We certainly are at a modern day Wright Brothers moment in time.

About Dean Polley

Dean Polley spent 26 years of his career in industrial and corporate Information Technology, ten of which were spent in the Middle East. He spent two years in Saudi Arabia with Hewlett Packard, managing the Saudi Aramco account. In 2001, he launched Dubai's first commercial Application Service Provider. He headed up ITQAN, one of the largest IT systems integration companies in the United Arab Emirates, with customers throughout the Middle Eastern region. His last three years were spent as Chief Information Officer for the Dubai government's Dubai Holdings economic development subsidiary, Tatweer Dubai.

Dean got into the drone industry in October 2013, initially as a hobby, starting off with a DJI Phantom for aerial photography. He soon saw the enormous potential of drones and in 2015 founded Aerial Vision Africa, renamed as SSASS Holdings in 2020 positioning the company as a comprehensive provider of turnkey drone solutions.

Dean is a past President of CUAASA (the Commercial Unmanned Aircraft Association of Southern Africa) and was subsequently elected onto the Board of Directors of the umbrella body, CAASA (the Commercial Aviation Association of Southern Africa).

Contacts

dean@ssass.co.za

www.ssass.co.za

https://www.facebook.com/SSASS.Holdings

www.linkedin.com/company/ssass

What Can AI And Drones Do?

Godfrey Nolan

There's been a lot of hype over the past few years about both drones and Artificial Intelligence or AI. In this article we're going to look at what exactly AI means for drones. We'll talk about what's happening now and take a peek at what may happen in the near future.

Innovations help the human race by automating manual tasks that were often laborious and inefficient. From the printing press to the electric light to the Lotus 1-2-3 spreadsheet, when new technologies are introduced, we see a massive jump in productivity. Drones are the equivalent of the 80's IBM PC and Apple Mac II. And mobile applications for drones are today's Lotus 1-2-3. When drones are combined with new AI applications, we're going to see a similar jump in efficiency with many more manual tasks being automated.

These automated drones will be utilized in many different industries, including Agriculture, Construction, Shipping, Railways, Warehouses, Healthcare and Energy to name just a few. These industries and more are going to see dramatic changes in their day to day operations over the coming decade. Drones together with AI are good at counting, measuring, identifying things or reading text and it doesn't matter if what you're looking at is moving or not. If you want an automated security guard, want to count crops or cattle, identify defects in a solar panel, read barcodes off boxes in a warehouse or read the text on the side of a shipping container, you can already do that and more from the comfort of your office.

Different Types Of AI

What exactly do we mean when we say AI in this domain? Are we talking about obstacle avoidance, or follow-me functionality or are we talking about computer vision? In most cases, it's a combination of Machine Learning (ML) together with Computer Vision (CV). ML allows us to use image classification and object detection to identify someone or something. And CV allows us to split the video into images and then apply our ML models against the video that the drone camera is capturing and display the results in real time.

Traditional programming is analogous to a recipe. You create a list of things to do in a specific order and assuming you make no mistakes out pops a cake every time you run the program. Of course, there are different styles and languages in traditional programming, but they're just variations on a theme. The order and how you group the ingredients and instructions may change but it's still just a recipe.

Machine Learning is a completely different type of programming. Instead of a procedural approach we teach or train the computer to pattern match. Thousands of pictures are used to tell the computer to recognize a cow. So later on, when the drone camera flies over a cow, the computer will say hold on, I've seen that before, that's a cow. It's also not exactly the same each time. The same cake does not pop out every time you run the program. It will be slightly different, a little bit smaller or a little bit bigger.

Putting Theory Into Practice

Machine Learning uses neural networks which are multiple layers of nodes. We tell the model what the inputs are and what the outputs are. Over a period of time, the network or model learns what outputs to expect depending on the inputs. Or to put it another way, it learns to predict the outputs based on what inputs it's given. We present a trained model with an image, and it will output what it thinks it sees based on the previous training.

To show you what the TensorFlow code looks like, the following is a simple TensorFlow model from a Google Codelab that takes the MNIST database of letters and numbers as its input and will then be able to predict what letter or number it is later presented with.

```
model = tf.keras.models.Sequential ([

tf.keras.layers.Flatten(input_shape=(28, 28)),

tf.keras.layers.Dense (128, activation='relu'),

tf.keras.layers.Dropout (0.2),

tf.keras.layers.Dense (10)

])
```

We define the sequential model as having an input image size of 28×28 pixels. It uses a multi-layer neural network, with a 128-node first layer and a 10-node second layer. The rectified linear activation function or relu is a function that will output the input directly if it is positive, otherwise, it will output zero. The dropout helps make sure we don't overfit the model so it learns correctly and doesn't get stuck in the training.

I show this not to complicate things, but to illustrate that programming in TensorFlow is all about making sure the inputs are the correct shape, choosing the models and layer, and then setting parameters to make sure the model is as efficient as possible. We are not creating the neural network.

There are four stages in Machine Learning, including Labeling, Training, Testing and Deploying. As an example, it might help to talk about a real application we created to count cattle. We used 5,000 images to train the model or neural network. These images came from the drone's camera flying over many different herds of cattle. We collected images of cows in Ireland, Romania, South Africa, Australia and several states here in the US.

The weather conditions ranged from very hot, to rainy and some images were even taken in light snow. We also flew the drone at different times of day to capture many lighting conditions. A box is then drawn around each of the cows in each of the images. This is what we call labeling. It's important to get as many different conditions, as many different breeds and as many different images to train your network. It's also very important to make sure the boxes are drawn as accurately as possible, and that there are no mistakes such as boxes around any other types of animals or humans.

To train the model, we use a framework from Google called TensorFlow. There are also other options like PyTorch from Facebook. These frameworks mean we don't have to create our own neural network, we can simply use someone else's. The act of training, then becomes choosing the framework. For models that detect objects, compare TensorFlow vs. PyTorch or COCO vs Yolo V5, then figure out how to add the labeled images. We feed the images and the coordinates of the boxes to train our pre-existing model. Training can take hours or sometimes even days depending on the number of images and the speed of your computer. It's best to do all the number crunching in the cloud on Colab or Google Cloud Platform where you can get access to large numbers of GPUs or TPUs to speed up the process.

Note that 70% of our images are used to train the model and the remaining 30% are used to test how good our model is at recognizing, in this case, cows. The test images will give us a good idea of how well the model will work in the real world. Machine Learning is also an iterative process, so we need to train, test and repeat. We do this until we get the highest percentage of cows recognized in our tests.

Finally, we need to deploy it. Since this is a drone app, we need to export our optimized trained model in a format for Android or iOS which we can use together with the drone. Fortunately, recent changes in TensorFlow makes this very straightforward, and we simply export the trained model in what is known as a TensorFlow Lite format. We can then import the TensorFlow Lite model into the Android Studio IDE which will auto-generate all the methods and functions you need to detect objects in the drone's video stream.

This is known as Edge Detection or Edge AI where the mobile app will identify any objects for which it's been trained in real time on your phone. You may also want to deploy your new mobile app on Google Play or iTunes so that others can download the app and count their own cows, sheep, crops or whatever you programmed. We also went one step further and allowed the user to create an automated flight, which took a picture at a number or intervals or waypoints so when we finished the flight, we had a giant picture of the entire pasture or field. We then used the same algorithm to get a count of all the cows in all the images in what is known as stitching. Typically, this is not done on the mobile phone but in a cloud server at a later point.

AI Drone Limitations

It would be wrong to suggest there aren't obstacles to overcome with AI drones. There are still only a handful of companies and projects that combine AI and drones.

Mostly, these are for transmission line or wind turbine inspections where the drone looks for problems on the powerline or cracked turbine blades. Data collection and labeling remains a big task. Sometimes, if you're lucky, someone already has a database of labeled images. A good place to start is TensorFlow's Datasets or TFDS which is a repository of over 200 unique labeled datasets.

If you need your own dataset, it's going to take considerable effort to get a good enough set of images to create an accurate model. While we got a reasonable result with 5,000 images above, a real application is going to need 15,000 images or more for a better degree of accuracy. Most drones also won't fly in adverse weather conditions, so if your security system can't fly then you're going to need backup security guards.

Finally, drones have a very limited flight time, and any automated flight will need multiple batteries, so they're not fully automated as yet.

AI And Drones, In Summary

AI and drones are very complimentary technologies. Although there are flight time limitations with the current drones on the market, battery technology is rapidly advancing by leaps and bounds. And, while there are also issues finding or creating a labeled dataset, there have been recent advancements in using computer generated synthetic datasets which are very promising. In a few years expect to see a large number of outdoor and indoor manual tasks being automated by drones. Most of the work it will replace are mundane, labor intensive tasks more suited to computers. Ultimately, this will free up humans to do much more interesting work.

About Godfrey Nolan

Godfrey Nolan is President of RIIS LLC, a web and mobile development company based in Troy, MI that specializes in mobile applications for drones. He is the author of six books on mobile development and security. He is also currently an adjunct professor at University of Detroit Mercy and SVSU where he teaches Mobile Development.

Contacts

https://www.riis.com

@godfreynolan

https://www.linkedin.com/in/godfrey-nolan

godfrey@riis.com

Red Lorry, Yellow Lorry
And Submarines In The Sky

Justin Melman

*This article has been dedicated to the memory of
Brigadier General Charles 'Chuck' Yeager.
An exceptional pioneer Aviator… and source of quotation.*

The title is certainly in line with the occurrences of 2020, so let's hope this chapter eventually makes more sense to you than Politicians being confused as Medical Professionals, Elon Musk's sons name, Viruses being man-made and Bat eating Pangolins on a menu. And what a year 2020 was…

So saddle up, the Dumb DFE is back with more thoughts, don't worry it doesn't hurt me to think, that much.

Let's be honest, we don't feel like we have longer than three minutes to watch an informative video these days, let alone feel like we have the luxury of enough time to read a book. So well done on getting this far. I'll also try be as blunt and direct as possible, without mincing any words. Please just embrace the sarcasm, intended humour and most definitely the late Great Chuck Yeager quotes along the way, because:

"You may be cool, but you'll never be Chuck Yeager with a Corvette and an F-20 Tigershark cool. Take away the car and the plane, and still nobody's as cool as Yeager." ~ Source Unknown

Chuck Yeager and F-20 Tigershark - Courtesy Northrupp Grumann

Here goes…

"Flight Planning is very important, do not neglect it. Fatigue is very dangerous for Pilots, do not ignore this." ~ Me, I said this.

OK, feel free to continue reading or go back to YouTube.

Still here? Great…

I have the privilege (as are all Pilot licenses) to test between 150 – 200 Remote Pilot License holders in South Africa, for their Initial Skills Tests and Revalidation Skills Tests, a year. I also inherited my Father's amazing skill of being able to not easily remember people's names, just to keep things interesting (if you keep quiet for about 3 seconds and you'll be able to hear my eyeballs rolling up into the back of my skull and hand slapping my forehead).

Ours (South Africa) is quite possibly the most heavily regulated country in terms of Part 101 drone law, in the world. The requirements for a Skills Test to obtain or maintain a South African license is in line with the tests required to at least obtain and maintain a Private Pilot License. However, the billing method for drone licenses is better suited to purchasing a six pack of beer than earning a Private Pilot License (PPL) the age-old way in that you pay per lesson and per flight. During PPL training if you fail a lesson or flight, you keep paying until you pass. With drone licenses not following the conventional method of billing, problems come to light in which flight schools are made to feel like they owe students their licenses. Just like going to the grocery store, selecting an item, paying for it and walking out of the store with it, receipt in hand and mask hanging off your ear. The only thing we earned was the money to pay for the item and desperate need to use hand moisturiser as a result of all the hand sanitizer blasted onto our extremities.

The problem then becomes one of attitude affecting aptitude. It does not help that this also can cause flight schools to turn into the proverbial sausage factory in order to keep the lights on, let alone turn a profit. Once that happens (sausage factory mentality) and flight schools start to fight a battle of survival, we see standards and quality drop and the simplest of regulatory requirements become ignored. As has become a trend lately, former students of those schools, are no longer eligible for employment at certain companies, simply because it would cost too much to retrain them properly.

One of the most important messages I try to get across to all sausages... I mean candidates is that, Aviation is language but it is up to us to know where to look for the puzzle pieces to formulate the larger picture. Where all of this becomes most apparent is during the Ground Evaluation Section, of the Skills Test, when a student must apply their learned theory to the flight planning process, through a series of questions and scenarios. Only after this, do we then go and fly the exercises.

One of the most common misconceptions I find as an examiner, is that completing the flight planning component is *just the pain in the butt homework that needs to be completed because I need to have something to show the Dumb DFE. All of which I will only ever need to use in 24 months for my revalidation.'*

To any of my students reading this… c'mon, be honest…

*"There is no kind of ultimate goal to do something twice as good
as anyone else can. It's just to do the job as best you can.
If it turns out good, fine. If it doesn't, that's the way it goes."*
~ Brig. Gen. Charles Yeager.

Just because the world might have stopped functioning as normal and at some points ceased to function at all, it does not mean that our learning should have stopped or mirrored what the world was doing. The world saw a shift in what an Essential Service was deemed to be and without going on a rant about wrecked economies, false heroes, induced poverty and applying sound logic to mass hysteria, panic can't always be avoided but it sure as hell can be managed with proper planning and understanding of:

- Your Mission

- Your Aircraft

- Your Equipment

- Your Surroundings

- Your Emergency Procedures

Not knowing how to deal with the above might leaving you feeling like Gen. Yeager did:

*"After about 30 minutes I puked all over my airplane.
I said to myself, "Man, you made a big mistake.""*

I don't think there's been an aircraft cleaning kit made to handle that yet anyway… All in all, consistency is key, find your flow, if there is a flight planning document out there that makes sense to you, use it. If you want to modify it, then modify it, if you think anything available is stupid then make your own one so other people can think yours is also stupid.

JUST MAKE IT MAKE SENSE TO YOU and cover the basics:

Work Out Your Aircrafts Maximum Range

Speed x Time = Distance

Use the Aircraft Flight Manual, Pilot Operating Handbook or User Manual (all the same things really) to find the maximum values for Speed and Endurance (time).

This will give you a maximum radius your aircraft could fly out to.

(See example below)

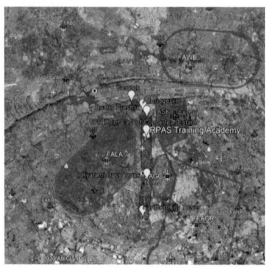

Legend:

- Yellow Pin – RPAS Training Academy

- Red Circle = 36km Radius from RPAS Training Academy

- Blue and Green Shaded Areas = Controlled or Advisory Airspaces

Yellow Points = Reporting points along Kyalami VFR

*ICAO Code Designators:

F = African Airspace

A = South African Airspace

Airfields Within The Calculated Radius

Some of the minimum details I plan for:

- Name

- ICAO Code Designator (where applicable)

- Radio Frequency for communication

- Contact Details (phone numbers to call in emergencies)

- Compass Heading from Take-off and Landing area

- Distance to Airfield/Airport

- Time it would take the aircraft to reach (at maximum speed)

Danger, Restricted And Prohibited Airspaces Within The Calculated Radius

Remember, I said *consistency* is key:

- Name

- ICAO Code Designator (where applicable)

- Radio Frequency for communication

- Contact Details (phone numbers to call in emergencies)

- Compass Heading from Take-off and Landing area

- Distance to Airfield/Airport

- Time for the aircraft to reach (at maximum speed)

Airspaces, Airways And Vfr Routes Within The Calculated Radius

- Names of areas to address over the radio

- Air traffic to be expected

- Alternative frequencies in case of emergency
- Joining procedures to be expected at airfields/airports within calculated radius

Emergency Response Plan

- Phone numbers
  - Ambulance Services
  - Police Department
  - Fire Department
  - Security Services

- Medical details of Pilot and Crew
  - Private Medical Aid (where applicable)
  - Next of Kin
  - Known Allergies
  - Known Chronic Illnesses and Medication being taken

List Of Procedures To Follow In The Event Of An Emergency

- Pilot Procedures
- Organisational Procedures
- Regulatory Procedures

Drone technology is the most wonderful thing, change is inevitable and with it comes greater access to revolutionary processes. It however still requires a back to the basics approach to understand and know what is around you, in the form of 'Situational Awareness' as well as having some sort of logical process in place to deal with emergencies.

I have flown in just about everything, with all kinds of pilots in all parts of the world – British, French, Pakistani, Iranian, Japanese, Chinese – and there wasn't a dime's worth of difference between any of them except for one unchanging, certain fact: the best, most skillful pilot has the most experience."
~ Another punch in the truth gut from the General.

The more we do, the better we become. Same with flight planning, Red Lorry, Yellow Lorry. As humans, the more we practise the fewer mistakes we make, the fewer mistakes we make, the quicker we become. Don't believe me, then say it over and over. Red Lorry, Yellow Lorry…

"Failing to plan is planning to fail." ~ Every Flight Instructor worth a damn, ever and another humdinger from the General, *"The best pilots fly more than the others; that's why they're the best."* Now apply that thinking to your flight planning.

Flight planning and fatigue may only have the smallest of connections in the conventional sense but let's not get Political here and instead use logic to delve deeper into the thought process that actually reveals more than we previously thought.

An emergency is not necessarily a panic inducing situation if you have reasonable procedures in place. It is however our obligation to avoid finding ourselves in such a position in which we have failed to consider obvious risks and hazards within our area of operations. One thing candidates always seem to forget is Wi-Fi and other signal interferences… so don't you go and forget that too.

Should any future students or Pilots needing Initial or Revalidation tests with me be reading this, here's a little ace up your sleeve… I give candidates a scenario in which their aircraft is experiencing a fly-away. I then ask the candidate to use the flight planning they have compiled to manage the emergency. Some days, I'll throw in a medical emergency while all of this is going on. The Joker in the pack you got your ace from… Return to Home (RTH) does not work. Save the aircraft, the public, other aircraft and ultimately the world!!!… not to be overly dramatic or anything.

Now throw that into a Beyond Visual Line of Sight (BVLOS) setting with the aircraft well beyond the reaches of the average human eyeball…

And then imagine that all happens on the last flight of your 12 hour night shift, five minutes before you're supposed to land and pack up. Geez… you might start to think I'm a sadist…

If you haven't considered any of this, then run through any basic scenario in your mind and use what you already have to deal with the emergency. If you reach a point of failure, research, adapt and re-run the scenario until you get it right. Then move on to the next one. Train your brain, sausage.

One thing to understand with all our automation lately, is that flight planning programs and flight management software, cannot replace the need for good old situational awareness on a pilot's part. Even if you can plan a drones mission to within an inch of its computational power and capability, there are two words that will ruin your extremely well planned day, 'Aircraft Incursion' …and 'bad weather' …OK, so maybe a few more like:

- Pilot or Crew incapacitation

- Loss of Command and Control (C2) Link

- Aircraft fly away

- Mid-air Collision

- Loss of telemetry due to interference

- Aircraft Incursion into your Area of Operation

- Public/Criminal Element incursion into your Area of Operation

- Loss of motor power

- Loss of orientation

- Rabid bands of terrorist children

- I was just checking to see if you were still paying attention

…and others.

Exhaustion and fatigue is the by-product of bad Crew Resource Management. Flight Planning should include measures to avoid running yourself or your staff ragged. As with all the titles and sayings invented during 2020, like babies conceived during lockdown being known as 'Coronials', there is such thing as 'Covid fatigue'. Basically, work your butt off without much result or rest-in between. So what saying could possibly ring true to us sausages failing to plan our operations adequately or get enough rest? Well, here's my favourite:

"There are far more aircraft at the bottom of the ocean, than submarines in the sky." ~ Forgotten sauce or joke book.

And in case any of you have missed this relevant quote in the best movie of all time (there's no arguing with me on this, you'd just be plain wrong and Top Gun 2 hasn't come out yet):

"A good pilot is compelled to evaluate what's happened, so he can apply what he's learned." ~ Tom Skerritt as Viper in 'Top Gun'.

Only to be topped by the General: *"If you can walk away from a landing, it's a good landing. If you use the airplane the next day, it's an outstanding landing."*

About Justin Melman

Justin Melman is still loving the Aviation Industry. Since penning the chapter 'Just a Dumb DFE' for Drone Professional 1, he has been to Somalia to train the United Nations in the use of their Micro Unmanned Aerial Systems (mUAS) as well as create multiple bespoke training programs for businesses and other government entities. Justin has also written articles for Air News International Magazine.

Having started Aerospace 3D in 2016, in order to focus on safety within the developing RPAS industry, Justin was able to combine his passion for aviation with his focus for safety within the aviation industry. Justin has vast experience within the drone industry with a massive portion of what he does being aimed at assisting companies and organisations in becoming compliant with the acquisition and correct introduction of aircraft and processes into their business. He does this by streamlining processes and facilitating the training and licencing of staff members on the systems which are to be used for their intended commercial purposes. Not just testing sausages.

Justin has also started focussing on online training programs, remote teaching and safety compliance items being available for purchase from the Aerospace 3D website.

Contacts

www.aerospace-3d.com

Linkedin: Justin Melman

Instagram: @aerospace_3d

Best Practice Guidelines For Minimising Wildlife Disturbance By Drones

Debbie Jewitt

Introduction

What a wonderful thing a drone is! Who can resist the thrill of flying and getting that bird's eye view? Drone technology is revolutionising a broad range of industries from the military to commercial and civil applications. Drones are now used widely in conservation, agriculture, construction and real estate, the essential services, customs and border protection, mining, energy, filming and recreation amongst others. Goldman Sachs predicted a $100 billion market by 2020 with an estimated 7.8 million consumer drone purchases in the same year.

This rapid rise in the number of drones has been a concern for the aviation industry, and legislative updates have battled to keep pace with the swift uptake of drone technology. Of primary concern is aviation safety and most of the legislation that has been developed has been to promote the aviation safety aspect and to protect people, property and privacy. However, the disturbance impacts of drones on wildlife is not yet well understood and as a result there is little supporting legislation to protect wildlife from potential drone impacts.

Certainly, many conservation authorities have banned the use of drones in Protected Areas or National Parks, unless duly authorised and permitted to aid conservation objectives. However, much wildlife exists outside of Protected Areas and it is in these areas where the greatest disturbance impacts can be anticipated.

Disturbance can be defined as the disruption of normal behaviour of wildlife in response to an external stimulus[1]. Drones can approach species in new and unique ways[2]. The stimuli from drones range from the low altitude of the aircraft, noise of the aircraft, and attributes such as the speed, engine type, flight angle, movement, size, colour and shape of the drone which could emulate the behaviour of avian predators[3,4]. However, when and at what levels drone disturbance becomes adverse is not well known[2] and will depend on the animal's anti-predatory strategies. Wildlife responses could range from hiding, vigilance, physiological changes, escape behaviours, or fight reactions. This could cause animals to move out of their territories, become exposed to other predators, alter feeding behaviours or, if breeding, impair the reproductive success of the animals. This is of concern for threatened species or sensitive habitats. If a drone is being used to monitor a species, then obviously causing the animal to hide, walk, run or fly away is counterproductive. Similarly, invoking an aggressive response may lead to an attack on the drone, potentially harming or killing the species and damaging the aircraft.

The fact that wildlife can be scared off by drones can also be used to good effect, however. For instance, the deterrent effect has been used for conservation benefit in Tanzania where drones have been used to chase elephants away from croplands. Similarly, drones have been used to scare off wild birds that cause crop damage, deter birds at airports or those which interfere with waste management[3].

Avian Responses

Most drones are flown at low altitudes making them likely to interact with wildlife and especially birds, which share a common airspace. In the southern African context, the greatest interactions between birds and drones have come from birds of prey, or territorial birds during the breeding season. Territorial African Fish Eagles (*Haliaeetus vocifer*) have been known to attack drones, destroying them in the process (Luke Wijnberg, pers. comm.). A fixed wing aircraft was attacked by a Pied Crow (*Corvus albus*) when the aircraft was on final approach, causing the crash of the aircraft and killing the bird. During multirotor aerial surveys of cliff nesting vultures, we had close interactions with African Harrier-Hawks (*Polyboroides typus*) and Lanner Falcons (*Falco biarmicus*) which dive bombed the aircraft but always veered away, at least in this instance, at the last second. Drones have been successfully used to monitor both cliff nesting and tree nesting vulture nests, with the birds showing little aggression but taking flight if the drone was flown too close. Indeed, conservationists have used a drone to successfully supplement the feed of a young Griffon Vulture (*Gyps fulvus*) after its mother was electrocuted from a powerline collision and the father could not provide sufficient food for the chick (Vulture Conservation Foundation). Very careful planning and airmanship was used in this case!

Some birds, for instance swallows and starlings, are merely curious as to the new type of 'bird' in their airspace and will fly closer to inspect but tend to maintain a respectful distance from the drone. Nesting colonies of birds, such as pelicans and Yellow-billed Storks (*Mycteria ibis*) were largely unfazed by the drone, which could be flown within 10m of the colony without causing flyaways. Our findings are in line with research in other regions where the greatest response to drones were from birds of prey, corvids (crow family) and larids (gulls, terns and skimmers)[5]. In general, larger birds and flightless birds are likely to show the greatest responses to drones.

Terrestrial And Aquatic Animal Responses

Terrestrial animals tend to be less reactive than birds. Disturbance impacts depend on the type of animal, life-history stage, level of aggregation, age, habitat and season[3]. For example, a fixed wing (SenseFly eBee) flight near a giraffe (*Giraffa camelopardalis*) cow and her young calf elicited a fleeing response from 80m away.

Three white rhinos (*Ceratotherium simum*) could be approached within 30m with a vigilant response, however this is very likely to differ amongst animals that are in highly poached or hunted areas and thus whether the animals are stressed or not, as well as the level of cover afforded by the habitat. Studies[6] on bears in North America have shown that despite a non-behavioural response to a drone, there was a physiological response (elevated heart rate), meaning the animal was in a heightened alert state. The heart rate spikes were correlated with wind speed and the proximity of the drone. Drones flown over crocodiles (*Crocodylus niloticus*) and hippos (*Hippopotamus amphibious*) caused them to move into the water or submerge when a multirotor drone was flown closer than 50m.

Marine animals, particularly whales, dolphins, sharks, seals, turtles etc, have displayed the least response to drone impacts with most species tolerating a drone 20-30m away[7]. This is likely due to the lessened acoustic intensity where the noise emitted by a drone flown at 10m was undetectable at 1m below the surface of the water[7]. Where drone noise is attenuated, for instance for aquatic animals or in noisy environments e.g., breeding colonies of birds, it is less stressful for the animals. Many species of animals use sound to perform a variety of life functions, hence noise pollution could negatively impact them.

In general the following flight attributes created the greatest response from animals: larger aircraft probably due to the perceived increase in threat and the probability of detecting the aircraft; flights directly towards or a direct vertical descent towards an animal; noisier aircraft (e.g., fuel-powered versus electric) and lower flight levels.

The response of wildlife to drones is complex and nuanced and the sensitivity species specific. Hence a precautionary principle should be adopted to minimise potential wildlife disturbance. The following best practice guidelines are provided with the aim of minimising wildlife disturbance:

Best Practice Guidelines [2,3,4,5,8]

- Take-off more than 100m from animals.

- Avoid manoeuvres above the animals.

- Avoid a vertical or threatening approach to a species, as well as sporadic flight movements.

- Avoid fleets of swarming drones.

- Monitor target animals before, during and after the flight.

- If you notice a response from animals move away or cease operations if they are disruptive.

- If a collision with a bird is anticipated, reduce speed or change flight course. If a raptor pursues the drone aggressively, land the drone as fast as possible.

- Favour low-noise or small drones against noisier or larger ones.

- Conduct missions as short as possible.

- Fly at the highest altitude possible.

- Favour lawnmower (parallel flight paths) flight patterns.

- Minimise flights over sensitive species or during breeding periods.

- Avoid drone silhouettes that resemble predator shapes.

- For nest inspections, fly at times in which eggs/chicks are out of risk.

- If the flights are around aggressive raptor's territories, perform them at day times when the temperature is low, and the birds are less prone to fly.

- Use an observer to report interactions with wildlife to the pilot.

- Use reliable, well maintained drones operated by experienced pilots.

- Select appropriate sensors and aircraft for the flight.

- Use safe flying practices i.e. identify withdrawal routes and emergency landing sites, consider the sun angle and wind direction.

- Adhere to civil aviation rules, environmental legislation and institutional animal ethics policies.

Be safe, be considerate and enjoy the wonderful world of drones and wildlife!

References

1. Weston, M.A., McLeod, E.M., Blumstein, D.T. & Guay, P.J. 2012. A review of the flight-initiation distances and their application to managing disturbance to Australian birds. Emu-Austral Ornithology, 112:269-286.

2. Wallace, P. Martin, R & White, I. 2018. Keeping pace with technology: drones, disturbance and policy deficiency. Journal of Environmental Planning and Management, 61:1271-1288.

3. Mulero-Pázmány, M., Jenni-Eiermann, S., Strebel, N. Sattler, T., Negro, J.J. & Tablado, Z. 2017. Unmanned aircraft systems as a new source of disturbance for wildlife: A systematic review. PLoS ONE, 12:e0178448.

4. Weston, M.A., O'Brien, C., Kostoglou, K.N. & Symonds, M.R.E. 2020. Escape responses of terrestrial and aquatic birds to drones: Towards a code of practice to minimize disturbance. Journal of Applied Ecology, 57:777-785.

5. Vas, E., Lescroël, A., Duriez, O., Boguszewski, G. & Grémillet, D. 2015. Approaching birds with drones: first experiments and ethical guidelines. Biology Letters, 11:20140754.

6. Ditmer, M.A., Vincent, J.B., Werden, L.K., Tanner, J.C., Laske, T.G., Iaizzo, P.A., Garshelis, D.L. & Fieberg, J.R. 2015. Bears show a physiological but limited behavioural response to Unmanned Aerial Vehicles. Current Biology, 25:2278-2283.

7. Bevan, E., Whiting, S., Tucker, T., Guinea, M. Raith, A. & Douglas, R. 2018. Measuring behavioural responses of sea turtles, saltwater crocodiles, and crested terns to drone disturbance to define ethical operating thresholds. PLoS ONE, 13:e0194460.

8. Hodgson, J.C. & Koh, L.P. 2016. Best practice for minimising unmanned aerial vehicle disturbance to wildlife in biological field research. Current Biology, 26:R404-R405.

About Debbie Jewitt PhD

Debbie Jewitt is a conservation scientist and works for Ezemvelo KZN Wildlife, the provincial conservation authority for KwaZulu-Natal, South Africa. She holds a PhD from the University of the Witwatersrand. Through her research, Dr Jewitt seeks to understand global threats, such as land cover change and climate change, and their impacts on  biodiversity and seeks solutions to these threats. She is the Immediate Past President of the Grassland Society of Southern Africa, an Associate Editor for the African Journal of Range and Forage Science and a visiting Researcher at the University of the Witwatersrand, School of Animal, Plant and Environmental Sciences. She is a qualified drone pilot and is responsible for rolling out the drone programme for her organisation.

Contacts

https://www.researchgate.net/profile/Debbie_Jewitt

https://www.linkedin.com/in/dr-debbie-jewitt-2a847496

Twitter: @DJEWITT1

Affiliations

• School of Animal, Plant and Environmental Sciences, University of the Witwatersrand, Private Bag X3, Johannesburg, WITS 2050.

• Conservation Research and Assessment, Ezemvelo KZN Wildlife, PO Box 13053, Cascades, 3202.

UAV Technology Overview In The Global Energy Industries

Jamie Allan

The energy industries are global behemoths which are critical to our daily lives. Without the generation and movement of power and goods, the world's population would not function (at least not in any meaningful way): it really is that simple.

Therefore, when it comes to ensuring that the sectors within are taking advantage of new technologies to enhance their operations, as they seek to do across almost every single cog of their complex organisational and operational machines, UAVs have naturally been on the radar of many.

However, their widespread day to day adoption has not yet materialised within any of the sectors that are the subject of this article. This is surprising, some would argue, given the present and unprecedented focus on the environment; and even more so, considering that these industries are arguably the closest to the green revolution.

Yes, some geographies are ahead of others (and for a variety of reasons that will be explored) but we are not yet seeing the second-nature use of UAVs as we have done with rope access technicians or scaffolding, for example.

The rise of these machines has been slower than many anticipated, and indeed desired. Nonetheless, where they have been implemented, it has been with incredible and tangible success.

Within this article I will specifically discuss the use of UAVs, though commonly referred to as drones, in both the renewables and oil & gas (O&G) industries. I will provide, through expertise from my first-hand operational experience and industry knowledge, a fairly high-level insight for a broad audience which aims to inspire and guide those with an interest in the technology and its benefits within these key global sectors.

Renewables

With regards to this sector, I will be dealing mainly with on and offshore wind but will also touch on solar.

Background

The global wind industry is regarded as one of the prime examples of an inherently innovative industry: using an infinite, free and green resource to generate energy via turbine generators which, by their very nature, are designed to become more and more efficient at power generation, scaling up in terms of size and use across multiple types of site and location, for an ever more diverse range of clients and a growing end user demand.

Onshore wind is much more widespread, and I assume nearly all readers will have seen or driven past wind turbines ranging from single small, independently-owned turbines on farmers' fields for example, through to commercial size wind farms with many dozens or hundreds of turbines all spinning their dance to the tune of the wind.

Offshore wind is in a different league all together, with truly gargantuan turbines the size of skyscrapers (and growing increasingly bigger) harvesting wind power at incredible scale. This industry has become a bit of a gold rush, with many pension funds and traditional oil and gas companies diversifying into this arena for a multitude of reasons.

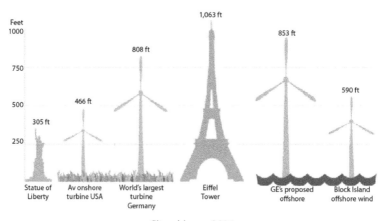

Climable.org 2020

Despite onshore wind existing on a recognised commercial scale for over 40 years, the first wind turbine built specifically for electricity production was by Scotsman James Blyth in 1887. Fast forward to 2020 and there are an estimated 400,000 wind turbines installed globally, including offshore.

Within this industry, tackling the operation and maintenance (O&M) activity of these vertical structures requires cranes, rope access, cherry pickers (known also as boom lifts, aerial baskets etc.) and even helicopters in some cases.

Methodology

Most commonly, rope access is the preferred method whereby technical personnel climb the turbine internally and, upon reaching the top, exit the turbine and proceed to abseil down the blades to carry out inspections, repair activity and other tasks. Understandably, this type of work is inherently risky (even deadly), slow and costly: not only due to the price of specially trained technicians, but also due to the lost production owing to the turbine being switched off whilst these activities are taking place.

Consequently, UAVs have been increasingly used to conduct visual inspections. At the professional level, this began from:

- a pilot flying the drone around the blade according to a data collection plan, with a separate camera operator manually capturing the required imagery, to;

- semi-autonomous drones which automatically take off, land and capture imagery, but still require an element of manual positioning of the drone, to;

- fully autonomous operations whereby the crew at site simply unpack the drone, perform the usual checks, 'press go', and the drone completes the full inspection of the three blades.

In all cases, the turbine has been stopped to allow the UAV to capture the necessary sides of the blades. Additionally, once the inspection was complete, data would have to be downloaded from the drone, uploaded and processed by AI, manual, or a blend of both, away from site.

Incredibly, from one turbine per day being inspected by rope access, double figures per day can now be achieved using drones.

Furthermore, paper and PDF reports have now translated into powerful cloud-based platforms which present inspection data in intuitive, interactive, and clear visual formats, providing asset owner/operators with vast data interpretation at their fingertips from any location.

The Future

The cameras carried by UAVs have improved significantly over time, allowing sub-mm resolution which results in more accurate defect identification. Location of the damage on the blade is continually improving with the use of GPS data and other sensors to within a few cm.

However, in development are new capabilities which would allow:

- data capture using high speed cameras whilst the turbine is moving (therefore eliminating downtime and lost production);

- thermal, lidar and other sensors, as well as the use of other types of UAVs, to increase the type and accuracy of inspection data outside and inside the blade;

- live processing of data and transmission from site using AI;

- more accurate repeat inspections which allow for predictive maintenance insights;

- additional tasks performed by the UAVs such as lightning protection system checks and other valuable tasks normally performed by humans or other equipment, such as turbine performance monitoring.

For the offshore environment, all of the onshore problems are scaled and compounded in terms of risk, cost, and efficiency but with the added complexity of a marine environment. Consequently, equipment has to be more robust, personnel have to undergo specific training, and data collection plans and risk assessments have to be conducted more thoroughly.

With this in mind, there are solutions almost commercially ready where autonomous surface vessels (ASVs) carry autonomous drones to the wind farm to conduct inspections. However, the cost of ASVs and associated risks of the marine journey are presently high and, in my opinion, present barriers to widespread adoption.

The logical next step, which I have been privileged to work on, are resident solutions located at the wind farm itself. Housed within a nest which powers the UAV and provides communications, the drone can be controlled from any location in the world and conduct autonomous or manually controlled inspections on demand or according to a schedule. By being able to avoid the offshore logistical and safety challenges (including easier Beyond Visual Line of Sight - BVLOS issues), whilst increasing the availability of inspection frequency and accuracy, UAVs are due to become integral parts of wind farm infrastructure.

Solar

A quick word on solar given its comparable simplicity to wind turbine UAV operations. In simple terms, solar farms are mainly located in open areas at ground level and require simple visual and thermal data collection to look for defective panels. Imagery can be compiled into a simple PDF report for the owner or transferred into inspection software as described above. Therefore, cheaper off the shelf drones can be used and, given the simple data collection requirements, present a much easier route into this line of work for pilots and businesses.

Oil And Gas

With regards to this sector, I will mainly be dealing with offshore oil and gas (O&G).

Background

In many ways the predecessor to the offshore wind industry, and therefore with substantial synergies, O&G has embraced innovation for decades and in particular another type of drone: the subsea remotely operated vehicle (ROV).

Whilst the ROV has in many instances replaced the need for divers, the UAV has not yet achieved the same with rope access engineers or scaffolding. Given O&G is one of the most risk averse industries around, it has been the case that owners and operators of assets, such as platforms, rigs, and floating production storage and offloading (FPSOs), require substantially more evidence of credible operations from service companies; this includes thorough risk assessments involving the offshore operations and equipment used, often to satisfy legislative requirements on the asset such as operating electrical equipment in or near to potentially gaseous areas.

Methodology

Much like offshore wind, O&G drone use is dominated by visual inspection and the desire for predictive maintenance, especially given the much older age and condition of the assets. However, the cost savings are truly staggering: for example, millions of dollars can be saved by using a drone to inspect a flare stack live rather than shutting it down for days and using rope access.

Even more desirable, and frequently necessary, is an invaluable digital twin of the asset. This is achieved and presented powerfully using photogrammetry from drone collected data, whilst augmented reality is also being used to tremendous effect utilising 3D models or real drone footage.

Nevertheless, the acceleration towards exploiting the benefits of other sensors and payloads is quicker in O&G, with existing capabilities and testing available in gas detection, offshore deliveries, internal tank/confined space inspection, lifesaving, asset and personnel security, and oil spill response monitoring, with resident systems also particularly suited to this industry.

The pioneering North Sea region has led the way with more widespread use of the technology over the years, followed, arguably, by the Middle East and United States, the rest of Europe and Australia, with much of Asia, Africa and South America still to take advantage of the technology on a greater scale.

www.transparencymarketresearch.com

The Future

Despite many similarities between O&G and offshore wind, the current societal focus on climate change coupled with the declining exploration activity for new fossil fuel resources and the move of industry majors, supermajors and engineering, procurement, construction (EPC) service providers into energy diversification (because of public perception, carbon reduction obligations and sustained low market prices due to globally slumped demand) creates a perfect storm with the ever ageing and deteriorating offshore assets for the rapid adoption of UAVs and, indeed, other robotics.

Consequently, expect to see greater tactile capabilities from drones offshore in addition to resident systems and, really excitingly, the increase of completely unmanned offshore assets (platform and vessels): all becoming the norm into the future as we strive to keep personnel onshore and out of harm's way as much as possible.

Entering Or Advancing In Each Sector

Drone and/or Drone Data Service Businesses

Onshore wind and solar have drastically lower barriers to entry and are therefore good starting points to those interested in operating in the energy sector; however, as expected, competition is fiercer with many service providers and lower differentiation.

For offshore work in wind and O&G, there are significantly fewer companies operating in this space but expect considerably harder requirements to be successful from both organisational and service delivery criteria: even manned aviation standards are stipulated by some end users.

Organisations Looking To Adopt Drone Technology

There are pros and cons to both integrating operations in-house and outsourcing to subcontractors, so make sure a comprehensive analysis of both is conducted.

Ensure you robustly interrogate and seek evidence of eye-catching claims from both service and technology providers, seeking external expertise to provide independent scrutiny if required.

Summary

What is certain is that we will see the increased use and capability of UAVs and the associated ecosystem within the energy sector to the point where it is no longer novel but the norm.

The opportunities for the technology to remove personnel for harm, enhance operations, and provide more valuable data are vast, but there are plenty to go around.

About Jamie Allan

Founder/CEO of Allan Panthera, leading independent and global drone consultancy, Jamie is a speaker at international events, trainer to organisations, advisor to global consultancies and investors, and has worked with INTERPOL on their drone framework.

Jamie began his career in the drone industry over five years ago as BDM for Cyberhawk, managing sectors including renewables, civil infrastructure, land survey, utilities and rail. He then joined an international marine business as Head of Global UAV Operations; highlights include the full commercial and project management of two award-winning, world first, offshore drone projects in two countries, as well as securing contracts with bluechip clients SSE and Equinor.

Prior to drones, Jamie worked for international O&G leaders IMI Plc where he negotiated a global MSA with Conoco Phillips, established an engineering facility, and grew the business 325%. He also served as CSO with Nor Sea Group, Europe's leading offshore logistics provider.

A lawyer by trade holding an MSc in Management, Enterprise and Innovation, guest lecture at the University of Edinburgh, and a mentor at the University of Aberdeen and Offshore Renewable Energy Catapult, Jamie holds a BSc Certificate in Risk Assessment, and has five plus years' experience as a serving police officer with Police Scotland.

Contacts

https://www.linkedin.com/in/jamie-allan-59a62445/

https://www.linkedin.com/company/allanpanthera

https://www.allanpanthera.com

Kurai

Clive Mathe

The beauty about the principle of writing and reading is in the communion between the author and the reader outside of time and distance; in the sharing of ideals and interaction of thoughts in such a beautiful way – in synergy – that always yields results and advancements that neither the author nor the reader could yield separately or even indeed working together (my assertion). The platform of 'books' is one of history's greatest invention and no other could incubate thoughts (which are things – powerful things at that!) with such great efficiency.

Truly, civilization has been propelled by a series of generations, each characterized by a combination of major and minor breakthroughs defining our social and economic context, and these forces of revolutions have been crowned with enough power to completely define how people live, interact and associate with each other.

It is truly remarkable, on how a populace manages to keep itself busy under the sun, and in the process search for the next layer of convenience that makes their lives easier, even by the slightest relative improvements. This natural instinct of a populace has been a powerful force to our progress and has allowed us to constantly take the tools that we have access to, improve some aspects of it, and leverage on other existing tools to form a new tool, whose efficiency and value is greater than the sum of the input tools used to make it. You should note that this new tool becomes available, through established mechanisms (the most efficient of which is the market place), and can itself be used as an input tool in the formation of an even more efficient one.

Through this devastatingly efficient cycle, we have indeed proven what is written in the Bible, saying in Psalms 82-6: *I have said, You are gods, you are all sons of the Most High.*

We have taken the earth as our canvas and beautified it with our creations. One such beautiful creation which has fascinated entrepreneurs, enthusiasts, and inventors alike, as observed around the 2020 timeframe, and certainly beyond, are semi-autonomous and fully autonomous unmanned aircraft systems (drones), whose value seems to be growing on a continual basis. For an Aerospace Engineer like myself, who spends time squeezing every last bit of performance improvement on aircraft systems, it is certainly exciting seeing the performance of the drones, and achieving flight envelopes that the great Wright brothers never dared dream about. The excitement is only second to the one derived from seeing the economic value these systems define, and a complete shift in the way we do things; and this is certainly true in more than just one industry.

Our journey started in a garage, usually at night after work, and on weekends, where I and my co-founder Sam would play around with all sorts of pieces of technology, and after figuring out how something works we would shelf it, and move on the next thing as typical engineering nerds who cared more for intellectual satisfaction than anything else would do.

It is actually more accurate to say that is where the journey continued – where it truly started would be decades back. In a small farming community where we grew up. There we would spend entire days at the fields doing menial tasks such as scouting for potential crop infections, crop spraying and applying fertilizer. This was a year round activity, and the harvests provided more than 50% of what was consumed at home all-year round. With such a passionate background in farming, what was to happen next when Sam gave me a call with ecstatic joy saying, "...Clive, I have figured out a way to use three of our shelved inventions to help farmers improve on their crop yields with a simultaneous decrease in input cost per unit yield..."; was almost inevitable, if not foreordained.

We founded KURAI®, an agricultural technology company that creates tools to help farmers with in-season processes, leveraging on drone technology, artificial intelligence (deep learning), and Internet of Things (IOT). Over 40% of potential crop yields are lost due to pre-harvest inefficiencies caused by uncertain natural inputs such as pest infections, and soil nutrition. This is true on an average African farm. To decrease the level of uncertainty and shift the scales of probability to our favor, it is necessary to convert most of the for-long-labelled "uncertain natural inputs" into tracked parameters. Furthermore, it is necessary that the insights given to farmers on a continual basis be coupled with at least the same level of process execution, equipping farmers with the means of acting on the already data-rich insights. KURAI® envisions this as the future of African agriculture, and we continually predict this future by inventing it daily, in both small and great steps.

A big part of this puzzle is the use of drones within the farming value chain.

We use drones to collect detailed multi-spectral imagery of crops. These images can have a resolution as high as 1cm/pixel, implying the possibility of having sufficient detail on each and every crop. Computer Vision (CV) and machine learning applications (working with agronomists) are then used to produce a great wealth of information that define value for farmers. The output from such an analysis exercise includes general crop health maps, early pest detection, inferred soil nutrient composition, and accurate yield estimations, but to name four. In the scenario described above, it is clear that drones are only but a piece of the workflow – howbeit, an important piece! Equally important, as aforementioned, is the data-driven action. We are able to use outputs from the analysis for variable rate and targeted application of fertilizers and pesticides. This is usually through the use of crop spraying drones, and smart tractors. In some cases, we have been able to realize over 20% cost savings on the farmer's pesticide and fertilizer bill.

Talk about leapfrogging the general lack of infrastructure in our African farms!

Perhaps the most interesting part of our journey at KURAI® was the transition from an engineering to an entrepreneurial posture. This comes naturally for technical founders, who generally are highly analytical, and apply first principles thinking to solving problems. This is very necessary in breaking down the problem to its core, to really question the assumptions established as constraints to value creation.

The second biggest problem for African farmers, is the general lack of key infrastructure, such as tractors, harvesters, etc. The third biggest pre-harvest inefficiency is the general low rate of value input from a farmworker into a farm. A manual worker can take over five hours spraying one hectare of land. On the contrary, it will only take a crop spraying drone just over six mins to cover the area, and it does it with unequaled accuracy and reliability. It is no surprise that the minimum wage for farm workers is the lowest in the country, currently at a minimum of R18/ hour (just over US$1/ hour!).

Does this then mean that farm workers are being replaced by machines!? Certainly not. This poses a great opportunity to upskill farm workers with the use of technologies such as drones. This not only increases the value created by one farm worker in a day (and hence a potential increase in daily wages, as some of that value is captured by the farmer as earnings), but also creates an opportunity for farm workers to work on other tasks that are more suited for human input other than, for instance, crop spraying.

When venturing into the drone business, it should be noted that there are many other general drone operational companies opening shops as quickly as many go out of business. Without a clear and sustained competitive advantage, you are merely trying to fill a hole in the market, and usually leads to rearview mirror behavior, always wary of what competition is doing.

In his book, *This is Marketing* (Portfolio Penguin, 2018), Seth Godin argues that in such a posture, you are driven by scarcity, and are only focused on maintaining or slightly increasing your market share. The entrepreneurial thing to do will be to take a generative posture, one driven by possibility, and not scarcity. This of course introduces an uncertainty parameter, as there is an associated incremental probability of failure, but if the prospect of success promises great value, the expected sum of value (product of probability and promised value) should be sufficiently significant to warranty your dedication to the venture.

From the very first day, we set KURAI® as an agricultural technology company, and not just a drone technology company (even though we designed and developed our own drones, but we did that sorely because we had the skill in-house and would certainly lower our CAPEX since we already had drone IP), and this distinction needs to be very clear when involved in the drone business.

Drone systems, as amazing as there are, are just tools, and they have to be treated as such.

For most of the applications, drones are data collecting devices, and the business cases arise from what you with do with the data. What we see with drone operators, especially those that solely rely on third party software for operations, is the lack of innovation as there are reliant on the efficiencies only provided by the service providers. There certainly miss on the opportunity to innovate around their offering, and this primarily affects their scalability, and at best they will just be fast-followers. This is okay if you want to operate at a certain scale and are content with that level of value, but if what you want to see is large-scale impact and industry-wide adoption of processes, you have to implement pre- and post- drone-use systems that do justice to the already great work that the drones do.

If you see it that way, that drones are just tools that allow you to collect massive amounts of high-quality data; that for true value creation, you still need to create high efficiency systems like any other traditional business.

This, of-course, will be to a lesser extent, if all you do as a business is just collect and deliver raw data, in which case such a market advantage will dissolve as quickly as salt does in boiling pure water. The availability of such a rich dataset also implies a great use case for an associated technology trend.

Machine Learning works very well with the availability of large datasets. Unless your tasks don't involve any data processing and/or analytics, it is logical to implement machine learning as part of your workflow. I do not understand any company that deals with large and rich datasets and does not enhance it by adopting such techniques to further add value to their clients.

As in any other business, it is your duty to walk every last mile to deliver as much value and quality to your customers as you can.

If you project a decade or two from now, you will realize that jobs such as for drone pilots will be obsolete, and the buzz about drones would have died down into normalcy. Like any other technological achievement, only a few would have greatly benefitted, and these are usually the early entrants (to a lesser extent), and the ones who can quickly see the trend and position themselves in the most probable outcome of events in the near future.

By positioning themselves that way, and effectively "betting for that possibility", they are in essence "buying that stock", and by the law of supply and demand, this increases the "value of that stock", or simply, the probability of that future position being attained. In this are President Abraham Lincoln's words true: *The best way to predict the future is to invent it.*

About Clive Mathe

Clive Mathe is a South African/ Zimbabwean entrepreneur and technology architect, and a founding CEO at KURAI®, an agricultural technology company that creates technological and engineering tools to help farmers with in-season processes. He was born and grew up in Zimbabwe where he attained summa-cum laude in his A-level studies, and moved to Witwatersrand University in South Africa where he studied Aeronautical Engineering. After graduation from Witwatersrand University, Mr. Clive Mathe worked as an aeronautical engineer and aerodynamicist at ADC – ARHLAC, where he was part of an innovative team of brilliant engineers that designed and developed the ARHLAC aircraft. Clive left ADC in early 2019 to co-found KURAI®. Mr. Mathe has a passion for using technology and entrepreneurship to help solve key inefficiencies and problems in the African continent, and directs his efforts towards both entrepreneurial and humanitarian efforts.

Contacts

clive@kurai.co

https://www.linkedin.com/in/clive-mathe-26a03159

UAS Categorization Model Adoption: A South African Perspective

Sonet Kock

South African Remotely Piloted Aircraft System (RPAS) Regulations came into operation in July 2015 and came about as the urgent need to regulate RPAS, popularly referred to as drones, was felt. At that time, the regulatory challenges posed by drones were a point of deliberation in almost every other country in the world with a number of different approaches adopted - from outright banning drones to simply ignoring the new technology.

Then ...

The regulatory framework requirements set out in the South African Drone Regulations closely resemble that of an Air Operator Certificate (AOC) and the operational control and oversight required are similar to that required by for instance a small Aerial Work Operator. Thus, in order to operate drones for commercial, corporate or non-profit use - a legal entity needs to apply for an RPAS Operator Certificate (ROC) as well as an Air Service License for commercial operations.

There are also regulatory requirements in terms of Remote Pilot Licensing and in the absence of certification and airworthiness standards, System Safety Approval is required for each RPAS to be operated.

In following this regulatory path – the then widely held concerns regarding public safety, security and privacy were addressed and the Civil Aviation Authority felt comfortable that it would be able to dispense of its mandate to not only protect people in the sky but also persons on the ground.

... And Now

But fast forward five years and there are fewer than a 100 Legal Operators with a larger number of applicants waiting in the wings. The number of legal operators in South Africa (SA) seems very low when compared to the number of commercial operators listed in, for instance the UK, New Zealand or Australia - but in order to compare apples with apples we need to understand that the Concept of Operations (CONOPS)[1] and typical Operations Specification (OpSpec)[2] within the South African environment allows for advanced high risk drone operations such as:

- Beyond Visual Line of Sight;

- Night Operations;

- Operations in Controlled Airspace;

- Operations above 400ft; and

- Operations with drones weighing more than 20kg.

Many of these operations are not approved for the vast majority of listed operators in other countries and those operators would need additional once-off permissions and waivers to conduct advanced high-risk operations, which are often only approved on a trial basis.

Future Skies – Challenges Facing the SA Drone Industry

In performing a Regulatory Impact Assessment, we have identified a number of additional regulatory challenges raised by the continued adoption of drone technology in a myriad of industries. Nationally, we need to promote the socio-economic potential of drones in the form of skills development, employment and small enterprise stimulation.

The question thus is how do we stimulate the local drone economy – in other words, make the commercial use of drone technology more accessible to more entrants (the so called massification of drones), but at the same time ensure safety and security?

In addition, how do we create the infrastructure to regulate and accommodate a vast number of additional drone users? How do we regulate drones being imported on a daily basis and where a drone has been used for illegal purposes, how do we trace it back to the Owner/Operator?

The Drone Industry is therefore faced with the following problem statements:

1. Facilitating large scale adoption or massification of drones;

2. Future proofing drone regulations – thinking of Urban Air Mobility and drone deliveries;

3. Addressing socio-economic challenges in SA; and

4. Public security and safety concerns as well as privacy rights enshrined in our Constitution.

Proposed Solution: UAS Categorization Model
(JARUS/EASA/ ICAO)

Due to drone technology's disruptive nature, these challenges have been identified in most other countries as well and for the past 3-5 years the following international agencies have been coming up with possible solutions to these questions:

"Burdensome and disproportional regulation would most probably lead to the development of illegal operations, due to difficulties in enforcement given the very high number of UAS sold and the lack of understanding of the general public of the intention of the rules"

Joint Authorities for Rulemaking of Unmanned Systems (JARUS)[3]

"In view of the adoption of this new Regulation, the objective is to ensure a high and uniform level of safety for UAS, to foster the development of the UAS market and to contribute to enhancing privacy, data protection and security."

European Union Aviation Safety Agency (EASA)[4]

"The proposed regulations apply to all UAS users. This approach allows lower-risk operations to take place without burdensome authorization requirements, as long as the operator remains compliant with the limitations set out in the proposed regulations..."

International Civil Aviation Organization (ICAO)[5]

The proposed solution comes in the form of a Categorization Model for Drone Use with three categories:

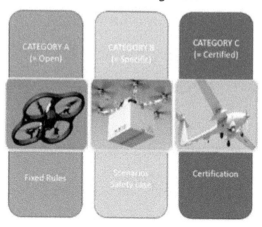

Fig. 1: Categorization Model (EASA)

Category A/Open Category/Low Risk Category

Safety is ensured through compliance with operational limitations, mass limitations, product safety requirements and a minimum set of operational rules.

Example: a farmer conducting an aerial survey of his/her crops in a rural environment - with little to no interaction with the Civil Aviation Authority.

Category B/Specific Category/Medium Risk Category

Requires authorization by a National Aviation Authority following the submission of a risk assessment performed by the operator. A manual of operations lists the risk mitigation measures or potentially the development of Standard Scenarios according to which the operation shall take place.

Example: a rooftop inspection within a suburban area – Specific Approval required from the Civil Aviation Authority.

Category C/Certified Category/High Risk Category

Requirements are comparable to those for manned aviation including certification standards for the RPAS.

Example: delivery of dangerous goods in a highly populated area within controlled airspace – continuous interaction with the Civil Aviation Authority.

An Adapted Categorization Model For SA

In assessing whether the proposed UAS Categorization Model framework could be suitable to SA, we can apply the underlying principles of Categorization to our problem statements as enumerated above.

1. Facilitating Large-Scale Adoption Of Drones - #Enterprise Adoption

Categorisation as a proposed regulatory framework is operation centric, proportionate, risk- and performance based.

Aims to strike a balance between establishing a proportionate regulatory framework and fostering innovation and growth.

Basic regulations are in place and the Categorization Model principles can be used to supplement existing regulations.

Guidelines to be drafted for the regulatory amendments required to implement this and ensure that risk is minimized but innovation is encouraged.

2. Futureproofing Drone Regulations - #4IR and Future Cities

A Categorization Model allows for developing proportionate regulatory framework that is flexible and futureproofed.

Applicability of proposed framework to be determined by

a thorough Regulatory Impact Assessment as part of drafting new regulations.

Drones play an integral role in future tech - develop Drone Regulations for a rapidly expanding industry taking into consideration the current and continued development of commercial drones.

Regulating new technologies is a cumbersome task – innovation is much faster than bureaucratic 'red tape' and the amended regulatory framework needs to be flexible and futureproofed.

Flexible regulations are required that keep up with technological advances to continuously benefit the economy.

3. Tackling Socio-Economic Challenges - #Drones for Good

Harness the economic, social and scientific potential of this technology.

Take advantage of the role drones can play in addressing Socio-Economic issues e.g., Public Sector services, Search and Rescue, Disaster Response and other Humanitarian needs.

Maximize the potential of the drone industry e.g., job creation, skills development and economic growth.

4. Security and Privacy Concerns - #Safe Drone

Public acceptance of massification of drones especially in terms of assuaging public security and privacy concerns is essential.

Preliminary discussions at Industry level will encourage the engagement of State Agencies and related Stakeholders followed by Public participation as required.

In further considering whether the adoption of the Categorization Model is a suitable solution for SA, we need to take cognizance of the existing legislative environment and in particular existing Legal Operators (ROC holders). In contrast to other countries where drone rules have been haphazardly implemented, the existence of a mature Drone Regulatory framework in SA prevents a simple copy and paste of the EASA or JARUS Models.

As previously stated, these SA Drone Operators already operate within the Medium to High-risk Categories. In my opinion, the current SA Drone Regulations fit in between Category B (Specific / Medium Risk Category) and Category C (Certified/High Risk Category) if we strictly follow the JARUS and EASA Categorization Models.

It is my suggestion that we incorporate the existing Drone Regulations into the proposed Model framework by adding a fourth category in between Category B and Category C to:

- accommodate the current Drone Regulatory framework in SA;

- reduce the impact on and disruption to existing Legal Operators; and

- facilitate easier access to more new entrants wishing to operate in the Low-Risk Category.

Fig. 2: Adapted Categorization Model

Industry feels confident that the adoption of a fit-for-purpose customized Categorization Model could go a long way in addressing the identified challenges.

Digital Drone Roadmap

The following Roadmap is currently being followed to link identified Objectives and Gaps to required Action Items and Activities in considering the adoption of a Categorization Model into the SA Drone Regulations.

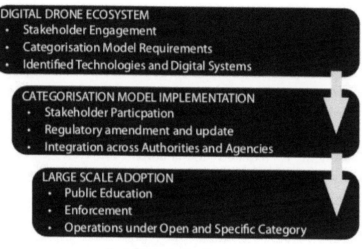

Fig. 3: Categorization Roadmap

Digital Drone Ecosystem

Industry has identified the Drone Digital Ecosystem that it believes will satisfy most requirements, when we balance socio-economic needs with safety and security requirements through the adoption of a Categorization Model suitable to our unique local conditions.

As stated previously - the key issue is striking a balance between establishing a proportionate regulatory framework on the one side and fostering innovation and growth on the other.

The Categorization Model takes this into account and allows for the development of a regulatory framework that is operation centric, proportionate and performance based.

Within this proposed system every drone which enters the country will be registered to an Owner / Operator notwithstanding the drone's intended end use (e.g., commercial, corporate or private). Please bear in mind that a drone used for fun (private use) poses the same safety and security risk as that same drone flown for a commercial or corporate purpose and, as such, both instances need to be regulated.

To support the mass proliferation of drones (especially thinking of cargo or delivery drones), a robust UAS Traffic Management System needs to be designed to safely facilitate integration into airspace. A digital or Remote ID for each drone is also an underlying technology required to promote safe and secure drone operations.

In summary, a technologically advanced Digital Drone Ecosystem is required to underpin and sustain future Drone Regulations based on a Categorization Model framework.

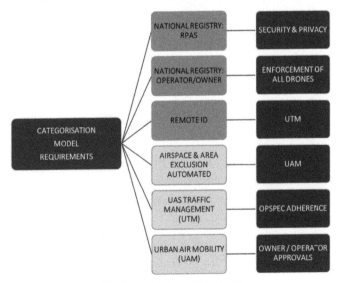

Fig. 4: Digital Drone Ecosystem

Futureproofed

Any attempt at drafting Drone Regulations needs to take into consideration the fact that drone technology is inherently disruptive - it evolves and changes rapidly.

Future regulations need to cater for operations by the Owner/ Operator offering a simplified commercial drone service as well as the not-so-distant future of Urban Air Mobility. This in effect tries to create a set of regulations that will cover a wide range of operations from private use by hobbyists with drones weighing <250g to dealing with autonomous taxi drones weighing >2,000kg.

With these types of challenges, we are forced to think outside the box and to come up with solutions that address our current challenges but that also attempt at keeping up with technological advances.

Harmonization of Regulations Across The Continent

A harmonized set of rules should make drone use more clearly defined and easier to understand to enable cross-border operations. For instance, a Drone Pilot License obtained in one Member State should be valid in all Member States to boost commercial drone operations across country boundaries.

Africa-wide there is the initiative with regards to the Single African Air Transport Market (SAATM)[6] that will be impacted by future cross-border drone operations.

The African Union (AU) High Level Panel on Emerging Technologies (APET) advises the AU on current and emerging technologies that drive Africa's sustainable socio-economic and structural transformation to position the continent as a frontrunner in the 4th Industrial Revolution (4IR). In 2018, APET published a high-level report[7] which considers drone technology for precision agriculture as a potential game-changer for the African continent.

Member States requested ICAO to develop a regulatory framework for Unmanned Aircraft Systems (UAS) that operate outside of the Instrument Flight Rules (IFR) International arena. ICAO reviewed the existing UAS regulations of many States to identify commonalities and best practices that would be consistent with the ICAO aviation framework and that could be implemented by a broad range of States. The outcome of this activity is the ICAO Model UAS Regulations[8] and companion Advisory Circulars which are intended to provide Member States and Regulators with internationally harmonized material based on the latest developments. It is foreseeable that several African countries will probably adopt the ICAO Model UAS Regulations which regulations are comparable to the Categorization Models of JARUS and EASA.

In Closing

The South African Drone Industry has been operating safely and securely since 2015 with a clean safety record. Important lessons have been learned during this time which can now be applied to the large-scale adoption of drones ensuring that all Drone Operators (including Hobbyists) comply with a set of drone safety rules which takes national security and privacy issues into consideration.

In order to further develop the South African Drone Industry, adoption of the Categorization Model is being proposed to augment existing regulations with the introduction of operations in the Open (Low Risk) and Specific (Medium Risk) Categories with the necessary safety risk mitigation measures in place for each risk category.

References

1. A CONOPS describes the user organization, mission and objectives from an integrated systems point of view and is used to communicate overall quantitative and qualitative system characteristics to stakeholders.

2. Operations Specifications means the authorizations, conditions and limitations associated with the operator certificate and subject to the conditions in the operations manual.

3. "UAS Operational Categorization", JARUS, JAR-DEL-WG7-UASOC-D.04

4. "Notice of Proposed Amendment", EASA, NPA 2017-05(A)

5. "Advisory Circular (AC) 101-1", ICAO, 2020

6. Single African Air Transport Market - AU Policy Document, www.au.int/en/saatm

7. "Drones on the Horizon: Transforming Africa's Agriculture", AU APET, 2018

8. "ICAO Model UAS Regulations", ICAO, 2020

About Sonet Kock

Sonet is the Founder and Managing Director of AviComply (Pty) Ltd – a consulting firm specializing in Aviation Compliance Solutions.

Sonet has extensive experience in Aviation Regulatory Compliance for manned and unmanned aviation and has been specializing in Quality and Safety Assurance for flight operations for the past 18 years.

Sonet is currently focusing on Enterprise Drone Adoption – the interpretation and implementation of the promulgated RPAS regulations to assist companies to introduce RPAS into their operations. Future aspirations include Drone Regulatory development and drafting, promotion of Urban Air Mobility and specialization in International Air and Space Law.

Contacts

https://www.linkedin.com/in/sonet-kock-1045501b4/

sonet@avicomply.co.za

www.avicomply.co.za

The Power Of Local -
How A Global Movement For Good
Is Changing The Drone Industry

Tawanda J. Chihambakwe

Between the year 2018 and 2020 over $1.5 billion in funding was raised for drone startups around the world. Less than 10% of which has funded drone startups in the developing world. In contrast, much of the drone testing, development and innovation by some of these well funded startups from the developed world are conducted in the third world, particularly Africa.

It has become commonplace for locals in developing countries to be regarded as lacking the knowledge, ability, expertise and capacity to innovate, deliver services and lead the drone industry development in their local context. This is perpetuated in both the public and private sector by government officials, the non-profit organisation sector, corporates and investors. The adage in the developing world that *foreign is better* is denying young startups and innovators in developing countries the chance to scale, access funding and be considered leaders in the industry.

With an emerging drone industry still in its infancy, the lack of investment funding and capacity building of local startups in developing countries only acts to widen an already wide gap between the developed and developing, regardless of the merit of the innovation. How do we close the gap and build local capacity and expertise?

What would it look like if we invested in and developed *The Power of Local*?

The Flying Labs Network is a global network connecting local hubs in countries around the world. With over 30 countries in the network, The Flying Labs Network has become the world's largest group of drone operators, technicians and data analysts using drones and robotics for good in social and humanitarian action. Each country in the network has one lab that is led by local experts who fully understand the technology and are able to deliver services, training and solutions through a tried and tested system.

The ethos behind The Flying Labs Network which the flagship program developed by WeRobotics is that local experts are best placed to leverage the technology and tackle local challenges. They have the local knowledge, understand the local language/s, and have the lived experience. Empowering locals to access new technologies, new skills and new opportunities, enables them to tackle problems more effectively, more sustainably and more inclusively. This is in contrast to foreigners who often take a top-down, exclusive and techno-centric approach to problem solving.

By transferring opportunities, supporting locally-led projects with best practices, workflows and guidelines and allowing access to collaboration, communities have all they need to manage their own solutions.

The aim of the growing network of Flying Labs is to build local capacity, knowledge, expertise and use robotics and drone technology for social and humanitarian impact. Guided by the UN Sustainable Development Goals the network has five main focus areas where the appropriate use of technology is applied:

AidRobotics

Through this, the Flying Labs work together to improve disaster risk management by developing policies, localizing drone and robotics solutions and response coordination in a manner that is safe, ethical and effective. This includes providing services and offering training for local disaster response teams on how to apply the technology to improve disaster risk reduction, preparedness, disaster response and recovery. Effective deployment of drone technology for Disaster Risk Management through the Flying Labs includes: Nepal, India, Tanzania and Zimbabwe where the local experts have delivered a wide range of solutions.

HealthRobotics

Under health robotics, Flying Labs around the world are involved in delivering much needed solutions for public health services in hard to reach remote areas by field testing and implementing cargo drone solutions. This also includes developing the policies around how cargo drone solutions for healthcare should be carried out in a local context as well as the technical and data solutions to ensure safe, ethical and effective application of the technology. Through its partners, the Flying Labs Network member countries have access to several cargo drone aircraft platforms able to deliver healthcare services in remote areas including emergency medical supplies, blood and other medical samples. In 2020 alone, successful deployment of drone technology and robotics for Healthcare by Flying Labs included Chile, Kenya, Nepal, Malawi, Peru and Ghana Flying Labs. Commercial drone service providers offering a similar service using drones in healthcare delivery include Zipline and Lifeblood who operate in a few African countries.

EcoRobotics

Food security, climate change and conservation are amongst some of the most pertinent issues we face in our world today. As a global network, the Flying Labs are involved in leveraging drone technology and robotics to help with ensuring sustainable agriculture and fishery practices, nature conservation and climate change resilience. The buzz words in agricultural technology innovation today include 'Precision Agriculture' and 'Smart Farming'. Precision agriculture in itself is an approach to farming that leverages technology to help farmers ensure that crops and soil receive optimum health and productivity. The goal of Precision Agriculture is ultimately to improve yield output and ensure food security in a manner that is sustainable, profitable and protects the environment. Technology used in Smart Farming and Precision Agriculture includes remote sensing data gathering tools like satellites and drone technology with the aim of helping farmers to make data driven decisions for farm management.

Using the expertise, knowledge sharing, world class professional training and access to the leading software and hardware gained through the network, Flying Labs are able to deliver various agricultural solutions.

Services and solutions include aerial mapping and surveying, boundary mapping, crop and plant health assessments, data analysis, crop spraying, pest control and aerial drone seeding.

YouthRobotics

The goal is to reach the next generation of young learners. Youth engagement is a key element for the sustainable growth of the drone industry globally. The aim is to positively influence the future industry leaders giving them ample exposure and teaching them best practices covering safety, ethics and responsible use of technology. These Youth training programs and Science Technology Engineering and Mathematics (STEM) diversity awareness activities are geared towards ensuring the sustainable development goals of Quality Education and Gender Equality. Youth Robotics programs are currently running in many of the Flying Labs including Zimbabwe Flying Labs which facilitates drone camps and other after school drone technology programs. The curricula and programs are tailor made to raise awareness about Science Technology Engineering, the Arts and Mathematics (STEAM). Training is conducted in person, online or both and involves giving the young learners theoretical and practical training on how to operate drones. Ultimately these training programs will be developed to not only teach children how to operate a drone but also how to code and program autonomous flight missions and how to assemble custom Unmanned Aircraft Systems (UAS).

A group of young learners aged between 7 - 10yrs old
after completing a Drone camp youth training program

Zimbabwe Flying Labs has successfully run several camps which have been well attended and reflect diversity with girls and boys alike attending. We believe that there should be more girls and women representation in this industry and are actively working to raise awareness of the opportunities that exist in the industry.

The Flying Labs also facilitate train-the-trainer sessions to build the local capacity of facilitators, teachers and volunteers who in turn reach out to youth in different communities.

Secret Sauce

The essence of innovation is that there is nothing new under the sun, just a different way of doing what has already been done before. The power of the Flying Labs Network is that a Flying Lab in one country is interconnected with all the Flying Labs in other countries helping the entire network to leapfrog the learning curve that independent drone companies must endure when they start out. Each Flying Lab has access to the projects completed by other Flying Labs around the world enabling them to use that as a model to localise it in their country specific context. One Flying Lab can access the entire project completed by another Flying Lab, from the proposal, to budget, interactions with local authorities for permissions and clearances in-country, hardware and software used for the project, data processing methodology, data output and ways to improve the project. This information is invaluable and ensures a high success rate of projects carried out by the Flying Labs because it removes the essence of experimenting or trying to figure it out without knowing what the results will be.

How are the Flying Labs doing this?

By Building Local Skills

The Flying Labs Network organizes and facilitates hands-on drone hardware and software training for various drone platforms and Social Good use cases. Training includes basic drone competency all the way to sector specific training such as flood area mapping or aerial crop spraying. Once trained, participants are assisted with their projects through advisory support for their projects. Working with different certification, academic and training partners. The format of the trainings include –Drone Pilot Training & Certification, Advanced Drone Operations, Drone Repair and Maintenance, Bootcamps for schools and universities, Disaster Preparedness Training, Simulation Training, and workshops for Multi Stakeholder Engagement around using Drones and Robotics for Social Good.

By Helping To Grow Local Drone Businesses

Growing the number and capacity of Drone businesses locally is important to the growth of the local drone industry. Flying Labs organize local Business Incubation Programs, facilitate project opportunities for local drone companies where available and rent out hardware and software tools to local entrepreneurs.

Flying Labs help share and create opportunities for local businesses, helping them build their capacity through high-value knowledge transfer and technology transfer.

By Facilitating A Drone Technology And Robotics Ecosystem

Working with diverse teams, Flying Labs collaborate with innovators, service providers, NGOs, manufacturers, academic institutions, community and the government to develop an ecosystem for drones for Social and Humanitarian Impact. The aim is to strengthen the local Drone and Robotics ecosystem.

Increase Impact

Individual Flying Labs coordinate and manage various projects that leverage drone technology and robotics to solve challenges in the humanitarian and social space. Projects include agriculture, disaster response, conservation, development and healthcare delivery. The Flying Labs support local NGOs and other institutions with advice on using drones and robotics for their activities and can even include hosting events and demonstrations to show how drones can be used for social and humanitarian impact.

About Tawanda J. Chihambakwe

Tawanda is a best-selling co-author of *Drone Professional 1*, an International Speaker on Drones and UAS systems, Licensed RPAS Pilot and Certified Drone Professional.

He got involved in the drone industry in 2016 when he Co-Founded Drone Racing Zim, an initiative to grow interest in the sport of drone racing. He then started PRECISION AERIAL, a commercial drone services and consultancy company with operations across Southern Africa which is a pioneer in providing sector-specific drone integration services.

He is also Managing Director of Zimbabwe Flying Labs, the local country chapter under the global Flying Labs Network. He leads a diverse team that is focused on growing the local drone industry through various activities and programs as well as delivering drone technology and robotics services in the social and humanitarian context.

A true drone development enthusiast at heart he shares his experience and knowledge on international platforms including speaking engagements he has been invited to at conferences and seminars in South Africa, Kenya, Nigeria, and USA. Furthermore he is a member of the Drone Council South Africa, a proponent of Drone and Data Ethics in Kenya and a volunteer advisor to the local Civil Aviation Authority in Zimbabwe.

He has a YouTube channel called African Drone Professional where he teaches people about the drone/UAS profession, drone industry development and opportunities in Africa.

Contacts

https://flyinglabs.org/zimbabwe

chihambakwet@gmail.com

https://www.linkedin.com/in/tawandajchihambakwe

YouTube Channel: *African Drone Professional*

Twitter: *@tawanda_jc*

Instagram: *African Drone Professional*

https://www.facebook.com/tjchihambakwe

Drone Crop Spraying in South Africa

Timothy Wise

PACSys was established in 2016 by a group of South African sugarcane farmers initially to research and develop incoming agricultural technologies. 'Precision agriculture' was the buzzword at the time and a variety of technologies were being touted to growers as silver bullet solutions that would significantly enhance profitability on their farms. PACSys' initial mandate was to research these technologies and their practical abilities to enhance productivity and profitability on farms.

The three largest full-cover food crops in South Africa – sugarcane, maize and wheat – account for approximately 3.4 million hectares of cultivated land. Timber accounts for approximately 1.2 million hectares. Due to a variety of factors such as terrain, size of farms and density of the crops – aircraft are usually the primary method of herbicide and pesticide application.

In sugarcane farming, aerial application has been the preferred method in South Africa for over 40 years but it is not the most precise, accurate or efficient method of application. However, it is used by growers in the absence of any viable alternatives.

In 2016, crop spraying using drones began to emerge, initially in the Far East, where the technology had been utilized in Japan, for example, for several years already. If drones could facilitate more precise applications suitable for South African sugarcane conditions, then we argued that drone technology could be used for any other crops currently using aerial spraying.

Reviewing drone spraying options lead to PACSys contacting with DJI, China, who manufacture approximately 70% of the world's consumer drone market (March 2020).

In 2016, DJIs first version crop spraying drone, the Agras MG-1, had been developed mostly to service the Chinese rice markets (small, flat and square fields). This model would have struggled to effectively spray sugarcane farms in far more challenging South African conditions. However, the fact that DJIs R&D resources and expertise recognized the potential of precision agriculture was extremely encouraging.

At the end of 2017, PACSys finalized an agreement with DJI for the sole distribution of their agricultural range of products in South Africa. This continues to be a highly collaborative and productive relationship.

The evolution of DJI crop spraying drones – the Agras MG-1S, MG-1P, T16 and T20 – represents a significant jump in terms of functionality and efficiency. The benefit for farmers is on two fronts. Not only are the drones proving to be far more precise and effective in their applications than traditional aircraft, but the rate at which the technology is advancing means the cost of applications are now lower. By contrast, traditional aircraft have ceased to innovate, and the application costs are mostly on an upward trend.

The challenge of South African farming terrain makes aerial spraying with traditional aircraft statistically one of the country's most dangerous vocations. On average, over the past five or six years, one pilot has lost their life in traditional crop spraying operations. Drones represent a safer alternative to traditional aerial applications.

From an environmental perspective, the drones fly lower, slower and more precisely than traditional aircraft. The risk of exo-drift (i.e. potentially harmful pesticide drifting outside the target spray area) is much reduced. Due to exo-drift, the South African Department of Agriculture, Forestry and Fisheries (DAFF) has banned a list of hazardous aerially registered pesticides for aircraft application, for example, in the challenging KwaZulu-Natal province.

Enhanced cameras and sensors on agricultural survey drones can also facilitate the identification and isolation of *hotspot* pest infestations in fields and farms. Once the hotspots are identified, smaller 'spot-spraying' missions can be programmed into the spraying drones to ensure only affected areas are sprayed. The resulting reduction in pesticide application obviously further reduces the cost for growers, as well as reducing the potential environmental impact.

Importantly, drone crop spraying represents a new employment sector. To meet growing demand, in 2019, PACSys established an agricultural pilot development program to resource various commercial drone spraying operations. Over 100 unemployed candidates were interviewed for the program. All candidates had either an agricultural degree or diploma but were currently out of work. This is encouraging because there is much talent emerging from our various tertiary institutions who potentially will find work deserving of their qualifications.

Had PACSys the resources to develop all 100 candidates interviewed, we would have. Appeals to various charitable and non-profit organizations for assistance with pilot development funding were slow, due mostly to there being no *proof of concept* up to that point.

In South Africa, all commercial crop spraying pilots are required to register with the Department of Agriculture, Forestry And Fisheries as Pest Control Operators (PCO). The road to full PCO registration for aerial application is long and expensive, consisting of several modular qualifications along the way. In 2019, essentially a start-up, PACSys risked limited resources and enlisted the first five candidates in the PACSys pilot development program. All five candidates passed and were consequently offered full-time employment as South Africa's first black commercial aerial spraying pilots.

Complying with regulations, has been a major hurdle for PACSys had to overcome in creating a market in South Africa for the crop spraying drones that will ensure growers benefit from access to this potentially farm saving technology on a large commercial scale. In 2017, there was no precedent for using drones for commercial crop spraying with the South African Civil Aviation Authority (SACAA). And so began a painstaking two-year commercial approval process which ultimately culminated in South Africa's first legal commercial drone spraying flight in September 2019.

We support the challenge bodies such as the SACAA, face regulating an industry as dynamic as drones. From a regulatory perspective, drone technology is evolving faster than regulatory reform. The frustration is drone applications can deliver economic benefits, but only once they are allowed to be used.

With the rapid advancement of the technology, the demand is growing exponentially. Since 2017, PACSys distributed over 100 crop spraying drones into the Southern African markets with approximately 50% of these sales in 2020 alone.

DJI announced the release of the Agras T30 version drone at the end of 2021. It represents yet another significant jump in efficiency that promises to further reduce operational costs. It also further widens the cost benefits between drones and traditional crop spraying aircraft.

DJIs has a strong commitment to the agricultural sector and the exciting future of the drone aerial spraying industry. DJI are also researching and developing other agricultural hardware solutions such as autonomous tractors.

For PACSys, it has been a privilege to positively contribute to a well-established industry. Our core objective is to drive a continental aerial spraying revolution – enhancing productivity, reducing costs, protecting the environment, creating jobs and ultimately to improve lives along the way.

Truly wondrous times!

About Timothy Wise

Timothy Wise is the CEO of PACSys and is a registered Pest Control Operator for Aerial Application in South Africa. Tim was privileged enough to be raised on a farm in the 'sugar-belt' on the KwaZulu-Natal North Coast and, after spending six years in London gaining valuable IT Project Management experience, he returned to the country  of his birth in 2012 to pursue passions for entrepreneurship, technology and agriculture. Often described as a workaholic, Tim's other passions outside of PACSys include sports, travel and the outdoors. An avid hiker, Tim has climbed Mount Kilimanjaro and now has his sights set on an expedition in the Himalayas!

Contact

https://www.linkedin.com/in/tim-wise-62580474

Marketing Your Commercial Drone Capability

Andrew Priestley

One of the benefits I got from reading this book was seeing an incredible range of applications for commercial drones. Debbie Jewitt PhD (see Drone Professional 2) cited Goldman Sachs who have predicted commercial drones would be a $100 billion market by 2020.

Since Drone Professional 1 was first published I have been lightly tracking the marketing of drone services observing what works and what doesn't. In this article, I want to explore how you might market your drone services more effectively.

From a review of 43 websites I identified seven themes.

1. **Product:** What specific core service is being offered (or services)?

2. **Inclusions:** What do they get, exactly?

3. **Target Market:** Who exactly is that being offered to?

4. **Performance:** What does the service do? What performance or results are being offered?

5. **Desire:** What is the exact desire the target customer is trying to fulfil?

6. **Articulation:** Have you crafted a sales narrative that is relevant and meaningful to your target customer?

7. **Testing:** Are you testing variables to find the hot buttons?

1. Product: What Specific Core Service Is Being Offered?

What do you sell, *exactly?* Several of the authors describe a broad range of commercial drone applications. In this volume the authors describe applications that include scientific research, site inspections, environmental surveys, surveillance and security, aerial photography, data capture and analysis, anti-poaching, education, manufacturing, health and safety, AI and robotics, and crop spraying.

But what do you offer? And what earns you money? It could be a bread-and-butter service. For example, several of the authors offer aerial surveys as the mainstay of their business.

Make your service offering list.

2. Inclusions: What Exactly Do Your Customers Get?

Simply, as a customer, what *exactly* am I getting? A one-off service? A package? A retainer? Consulting? What exactly do I *get* for my money? Do you have service menu or a rate card?

For example, a drone videographer has one, two and four drones available for half day, full day, week day/weekend services, post production, editing, uploading, campaign management etc. A security service offers nighttime aerial surveillance.

So, I own a farm and I want a land survey performed. What do I get? Does your offer include one, two or even more drones? Serious camera gear. Special cameras? Real time data? Drone operators? How many? Data analysis? Do I get a written report with recommendations?

List the options and specifications. And terms and conditions. And price points.

Most of the sites I reviewed were marketing their equipment list ... but it was unclear what options were available; and how I might determine the right option for me.

When I was selling preventative maintenance to the mining industry, a common problem was sending the wrong team on-site. We determined there were eight levels of service and created a customer questionnaire that would enable us to deploy the right team. We also explained how a client might determine their needs and craft a ballpark quote. How is it priced? What do I get?

3. Target Market: Who Exactly Is Your Service For?

Get as niched as you possibly can. As I understand it, Kim James offers aerial surveillance specifically for managers of residential gated communities (i.e., golf course communities) who want to improve the safety and security for that community ... *at night*.

Tim Wise offers crop spraying specifically for sugarcane farmers (although it appears that service offering will extend to other crops).

The majority of operators reviewed, market their services, *generally*, for *everyone*. It was confusing who would exactly benefit ... most.

Be specific. Niche down.

4. Performance: What Does The Service Do, Exactly?

If I get you to do a land survey, what does that mean for me? Exactly? You want to really dig into this question because most of the marketing I looked at gave me a shopping list of their tools and equipment. Warning. It doesn't work.

So, imagine that you are driving and your car breaks down. You ring up roadside assist and 40 minutes later the AA pull up. A guy gets out, opens the van doors, and says, *Look I got all these amazing spanners. I've 1/4 inch, 1/2 inch, 3/4 inch, 7/8ths, 5/16ths. And, I've got wrenches ... and screwdrivers - imperial and metric. I've got a battery charger and a jump starter kit. I've got a car lift ...*

At this point, what would you say?

Who cares? Get my car working! Get me back on the road!

The AA performance features might be: you get fast response. You get a qualified, knowledgeable mechanic. With tools. And they know how to use them. And you get back on the road fast.

Most drone services companies are selling the tool kit.

Make a long list of what your drone does. For me.

Let's pretend Tim Wise says the surveys are safer, faster, cheaper, more efficient, more precise and effective. And better for crop yields. It's a given the drone can do the spraying, isn't it? Do you care how many propellers his drone has? Or about the battery life? Or how fast it flies?

The editor, Louise Jupp wrote a book called *Precision Farming From Above* that spells out - *exactly* - the performance features of drones as it relates to agribusiness, and improving crop yields.

Let's say she offers thermal imaging and GPS-specific inspections at lower altitudes meaning faster identification of soil erosion or pest infestations, lowering crop damage.

Kim James paints a vivid performance picture for her clients. Let's pretend, increased night surveillance, automatic recording, better night-time face recognition - a proven deterrent for criminals. Gated communities are more secure. There's less crime. Residents *feel* safer. Residents can see visible policing and a physical presence; but so too, criminals. There are less insurance claims and lower premiums. The value of those properties go up and there is increased occupancy. And ... and ... and ...

Get a really detailed list of what your drone *does*. What's the performance? And what does that mean to me?

My review showed an absence of customer-centric narrative. The emphasis is on the gear. Selling the tool kit. I might ask about your gear, of course, but in reality, I want to know what it will do ... for me.

My suggestion is get a list of *at least* 100 performance points. Each one of those points can be repurposed as content on social media, your website or sales literature.

5. Desire: What Is The Exact Desire The Target Customer Is Trying To Fulfil?

My car breaks down. I ring the AA. What do I want? I want to check out the tools in the van, right? *No, I want to get going.*

I'm a farmer. I want to look at all your cool gear, right? No, I want increased crop yields.

I manage a gated community. I want a safer community.

Get it?

What's the thing that your target client *desires* ... most?

Importantly, you do not have to create this desire. *It already exists.* This was the central premise of the 1960s advertising genius, Eugene Schwarz' classic marketing book, *Breakthrough Advertising.* Well worth reading.

A big mistake I *still* see companies make is thinking they've got to create that desire. No. Wrong. You need to identify the desire that already exists ... *and tap it.* For example, the weight loss industry does not need to convince people to lose weight. That desire *already* exists.

What desires do your target customers already have?

The landowner wants greater crop yields. The estate manager

wants a safer community. Drone operators want to operate safely. Or legally. You don't have to go and create that desire.

The review shows the use of the primary customer desire is conspicuously absent. Most marketing is about the tool kit ... not what target customer desires most. The end result.

Spend a lot of time on this. List all the desires your target customer is trying to fulfil, that you can think of.

6. Clearly Articulate The Value To The Target Customer

So, thinking of your target customer, get your list of performance features ... *and* your list of desires. Then pick one item from each list, and build a compelling, articulate narrative around those two variables. For example:

Most estate managers in South Africa are worried about the crime rate and want safer gated communities. Specifically, increased surveillance at night that provides impeccable face recognition of perpetrators. You might want to talk to XYZ company. We specialise in ...

Of course, the solution is your version of drone surveillance.

My observation was no matter how long or short the copy - most marketing proposals fail to articulate the specific desire or performance value to the target consumer.

7. Test, Test, Test (And Test)

Be thorough. Be exhaustive. Test one *desire* variable ... against one *performance* variable. By the way, did you know you can methodically test all the variables in your social media channels, for free, or low cost? Why aren't you testing, then?

Keep testing for engagement. One of my clients tested 175 variable combinations before they hit the hot button and turned on the money tap.

This is the value of A/B split testing.

Contrast using the same proposition in all your marketing for the nest 12 months. That was one flaw in Yellow Pages advertising. Now you can test anything, anytime, 24/7.

Consider this: someone out there, without your gear, or knowledge, or expertise will out-market you and grab market share … simply because they tested variables.

That's what you want, right? If you aren't testing you are leaving money on the table. In my experience, a lot.

To Summarise

The key steps are:

1. Get super clear what product or service is being offered.

2. Be clear what the customer gets, exactly.

3. Be specific about who it is for, exactly.

4. Drill exhaustively into the performance being offered. Get at least 100 things that you're drone does.

5. Be super clear on what your target customer desires.

6. Craft a very compelling narrative.

7. Test it.

I hope that helps.

About Andrew Priestley

Andrew Priestley mentors entrepreneur leaders worldwide. He is qualified in industrial and organisations; psychology, is an award winning business coach, bestselling author and an in demand speaker.

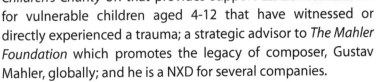

He is also the Chairman of *Clear Sky Children's Charity UK* that provides support for vulnerable children aged 4-12 that have witnessed or directly experienced a trauma; a strategic advisor to *The Mahler Foundation* which promotes the legacy of composer, Gustav Mahler, globally; and he is a NXD for several companies.

He loves to cook, draw and play music. He loves his garden and is a strong advocate of consciously caring for the environment wherever you live.

Contact

You can find him on LinkedIn or *www.andrewpriestley.com*

Book a 30-minute chat: *https://andrewpriestley.as.me*

Mind The Gap – The Opportunities The Drone Industry Offers As A Driver For Closing The Gender Gap In Aviation

Louise Jupp

Introduction

When I say *Mind the Gap*, I am not referring to the space between the train and platform that can catch passengers unawares, but the gender gap for women in aviation, and how we can close that gap.

Over the last 100 years, women have played significant roles in aviation and aerospace, – on the ground and in the air. Yet, there has been a persistent gender gap across all roles in aviation, from pilot, airline captain to engineer, mechanic, CEO, airport manager and air traffic controller. The main role where the percentage consistently swings in women's favour is flight attendant! This overall imbalance is particularly evident for the 'new kid on the block', the drone industry.

There are many similarities between manned aviation and the drone industry. One of the more unfortunate ones is the low number of women pursuing careers and holding positions of leadership.

It is axiomatic that there is nothing women cannot do in or with aviation. Moreover, as proven in many professions, the importance of gender diversity is undeniable. Numerous studies confirm diversity in the workplace is in everyone's interest.

'All organisations benefit from the richness of view, opinions and knowledge that comes from having a diverse culture'. This is also borne out by the bottom line; *'... companies with more diverse teams produce 19% more revenue.'*[1, 2]

Much is being done to address the shortfall of women choosing a career in aviation and, more importantly, staying in the industry.

Globally, there are multiple initiatives, programmes, organisations and progressive companies promoting aviation to girls and women, and yet the rate of change remains disappointingly slow.

Without doubt, the drone industry has a huge role to play in opening up all aspects of the aviation (and aerospace) industry to girls and women, by providing rewarding careers. It also presents an opportunity to close the 'gap' more quickly – provided that they are aware of the industry and see the achievements being made by women, **as entrepreneurs, role-players and in positions of leadership.**

What Is The Gap?

A 2018 study[3] which involved 112 drone services companies across seven countries, showed that 87% of their employees were men. The percentage of men in technical and pilot positions was significantly higher than women; whereas a higher percentage of women were employed in human resources, business development, marketing and other categories. Only 1% of women held positions relating to technical management.

The following table comprises selected data from the US Federal Aviation Administration (FAA) for December 2019. It illustrates the number and percentage of women holding pilot's licenses, including remote or drone pilot licenses.

Women Holding Pilot Licenses (USA)	2019	Aviation (Women)	Unmanned Aviation (Women)
All Pilots Category*	664,565	52,740 (7.9%)	-
Commercial Pilots	100,863	7,038 (7.0%)	-
Air Transport Pilots	164,947	7,503 (4.6%)	-
Remote Pilots	160,302	-	10,818 (6.7%)

Source: US Federal Aviation Administration[4]
* Excluding Remote Pilots.

It is significant that the FAA data shows that between 2016 – 2019 the number of women pilots in manned aviation increased by 1.2%, while the number of women remote pilots increased by 2.8%.

Clearly the opportunities in the drone industry are not limited to being a drone pilot, but this data highlights the potential for capturing the attention of girls and women and providing one of the entry points into the drone industry and aviation. I will return to this point in 'Closing the Gap' below.

Women Holding Pilot Licenses (USA)	2019	2018	2017	2016*
	Percentage of women pilots for each category			
All Pilots Category**	7.9%	7.3%	7.0%	6.7%
Remote Pilots	6.7%	5.8%	5.0%	3.9%

Source: US Federal Aviation Administration[4]
* FAA data for remote pilots is only available from 2016.
** Excluding Remote Pilots.

Why Is There A Gap?

There are many reasons for the imbalance in the drone industry, the most common being:

- A lack of awareness of career opportunities for girls or women.

- Dealing with stereotypes and attitudes held by both women and men.

- The preconception of having to be technically minded.

- A lack of role models, mentors or support frameworks.

Closing The Gap?

Drones are transforming commercial, agricultural, industrial, public safety, conservation, transportation, utilities, medical and humanitarian spaces. It is this transformation that offers more opportunities for women to become involved, if they so choose. For example:

- There are multiple points of entry into or using the drone industry, whether targeting a career in the industry from the outset; utilizing skills and expertise gained in another profession within the aviation industry; or by applying drone technology to other professions for commercial or altruistic purposes.

- Becoming a drone pilot is significantly less expensive and time consuming and, in many cases, less demanding in terms of qualifications.

- The 'return on investment' on obtaining pilot licenses, purchasing the equipment and implementation in particular, can be significantly quicker than for manned aviation, depending on legal operating requirements.

- The legal and safety frameworks for establishing commercial drone services and other related companies, such as training establishments, are far less complicated or onerous.

- Not every facet of the drone industry requires technical qualifications and expertise to be able to use drone technology, or, more importantly, benefit from its application.

- Drones are widely accessible and cheaper to purchase, maintain and use than aircraft.

- Drones are logistically more flexible in their application and, through rapid and effective data collection alone, offer powerful management and decision-making tools in a wide range of commercial applications. They are also providing delivery systems for medical logistics, agricultural spraying and seed planting for forestry and habitat rehabilitation.

The drone industry has been consistently attracting substantial investment, including software and specialised application of drone technology, such as agricultural applications, delivery systems and flight safety systems. This can provide important capital boosts for entrepreneurs and new start-ups.

Furthermore, drone technology can provide an exciting catalyst for attracting girls to science, technology, engineering and mathematics (STEM) subjects that can either lead to careers in the drone industry or aviation and aerospace. Clearly, the drone industry has already inspired the imagination of many from multiple different angles and disciplines.

Collectively, these features of the drone industry lower the real and perceived barriers to entry for girls and women. However, 'young girls cannot be what they cannot see.'[5] In order for girls (and women) to choose to become involved in or with the drone industry, it is critical to raise awareness of the industry, those already in the industry, the companies supporting diversity and inclusivity and the benefits of applying drone technology.

The drone industry has evolved its own suite of initiatives, programmes, networking and supportive organisations, collaborations of progressive companies and highly proactive influencers that are advocating the industry and the career opportunities for women. It may still be early days for a young industry, but indications suggest the overall signs are positive, albeit it with an apparent lag.[6]

Given what has been achieved thus far with attracting women in the short lifetime of the drone industry, there is every reason, in my opinion, to see the percentage of female representation, from the remote controller to the boardroom, reach double figures in the next ten years. This is further attainable if manned aviation and the drone industry collaborate with their activities to target girls in the classroom and so create a pool of empowered talent for the future.

Who Is Closing The Gap?

I have had the recent privilege of interviewing a number of women in the African drone industry for a YouTube video series I am creating for Women and Drones, Africa (*www.womenanddrones.com*). The purpose of the video series is to raise awareness of these women and their backgrounds to help provide inspiration and role models for girls and women in Africa.

These women are from a variety of backgrounds and age groups. Some have been drawn to the drone industry as a second career, are starting out on their drone careers or already have qualifications and expertise pertaining to manned aviation. Interestingly, some were initially targeting careers in manned aviation but due to various reasons were unable to continue. Then, as they say themselves, *drones found them* and their careers have advanced in a different but entirely gratifying way.

Furthermore, these women are already performing a wide range of roles in the drone industry, including:

- Entrepreneurs, company founders/ co-founders, owners, partners and directors.

- Operational roles including, manager, safety and security, quality assurance and communications.

- Instructors and Designated Flight Examiner.

- Maintenance Technician.

- Pilots (fixed wing, multi-rotor and vertical take-off and land (VTOL) hybrids, night flying and Beyond Visual Line of Sight (BVLOS).

- Legal, policy and strategy.

- Industry influencers and spokeswomen.

The range of uses of drone technology these women are involved in, include: medical deliveries, disease monitoring, education and training, agriculture, disaster management, security, land use planning and management, building local technology capabilities and drone racing.

A Call To Action

This industry has much to offer. I hope this article has sparked an idea or triggered a desire to investigate the drone industry further or even made you think of someone who might be interested.

I encourage you to take the plunge. Investigate what you can do within this industry. Research how you can take part or utilise this industry from wherever your interests may lie – whether technical, non-technical or from another profession entirely. Google, read, watch, attend open days and reach out to companies or organisations for more information.

I would also recommend you join a networking organisation such as Women and Drones (*www.womenanddrones.com*). Women and Drones are at the forefront of promoting female participation across the full spectrum of disciplines and roles in the drone industry. They also aim to inspire and support girls and women from *kindergarten to career* to pursue careers in STEM and aviation. Women and Drones provide a great platform for you to meet, network and learn from other women who are already in the industry.

This is an exciting innovative industry with the power to provide rewarding careers where you truly can make a difference, be a pioneer and engage with others who are passionate about their role in or with drone technology.

References

1. Korn Ferry (2020) 'Soaring through the Glass Ceiling: Taking the Global Aviation and Aerospace Industry to New Heights Through Diversity and Inclusion.'

2. McNabb M (2019) 'Why Women are Important to the Drone Industry – Voices from the Field.' https://www,dronelife.com

3. Kuzma J. & Dobson K. (2018) Gender Diversity in the Drone Industry. International Journal of Gender, Science and Technology UK.

4. https://www.faa.gov/data_research/aviation_data_statistics/civil_airmen_statistics

5. Bennett. K (2019). 'Getting the Balance Right.' Royal Aeronautical Society. https://www.aerosociety.com/news/getting-the-balance-right

6. McNabb M (2019) 'Why Women are Important to the Drone Industry – Voices from the Field.' https://www,dronelife.com

About Louise Jupp

Louise Jupp is the Amazon best-selling author of *Precision Farming from Above* (2018) and editor of the best-selling *Drone Professional 1* (2020). She is a South African Civil Aviation Authority licensed drone pilot and drone instructor. She has a Master's degree in environmental science and has over 29 years' experience in environmental impact assessment and management in the UK, Europe and across Africa.

Louise is the founder of Terreco Aviation, a consultancy dedicated to developing the professional use of drone technology in general and in agriculture and sustainable food production in particular. She believes commercial drone systems are fundamental to improving food security and meeting increasing food demand in inherently more sustainable ways.

Louise actively promotes the professional drone industry through books, collaborative papers, international speaking, as an advisor and as a member of several committees that aim to advance the use of drones in Southern Africa, USA and Europe.

Contacts

http://linkedin.com/in/louise-jupp

louise@terrecoaviation.com

www.terrecoaviation.com

Contribute To Future Editions
Of Drone Professional

Building on the #1 best-selling success of *Drone Professional 1*, and the response to *Drone Professional 2*, I'd like to invite you to contribute to future editions of *Drone Professional*.

I am looking for inputs from experts in all fields of the global professional drone industry, from educators and instructors, drone designers and manufacturers, software developers; regulators and air safety specialists, designers and manufacturers, professionals applying drone technology in their sector, legal specialists, accident investigators, sensor specialists to drone pilots and operators.

Please share your experience, case studies, technological and operational insights, best practice recommendations and business guidance and current best thinking or thoughts on the future of the professional drone industry.

If you would like to receive the *Drone Professionals Author's Guide,* please email me now at:

Louise@terrecoaviation.com